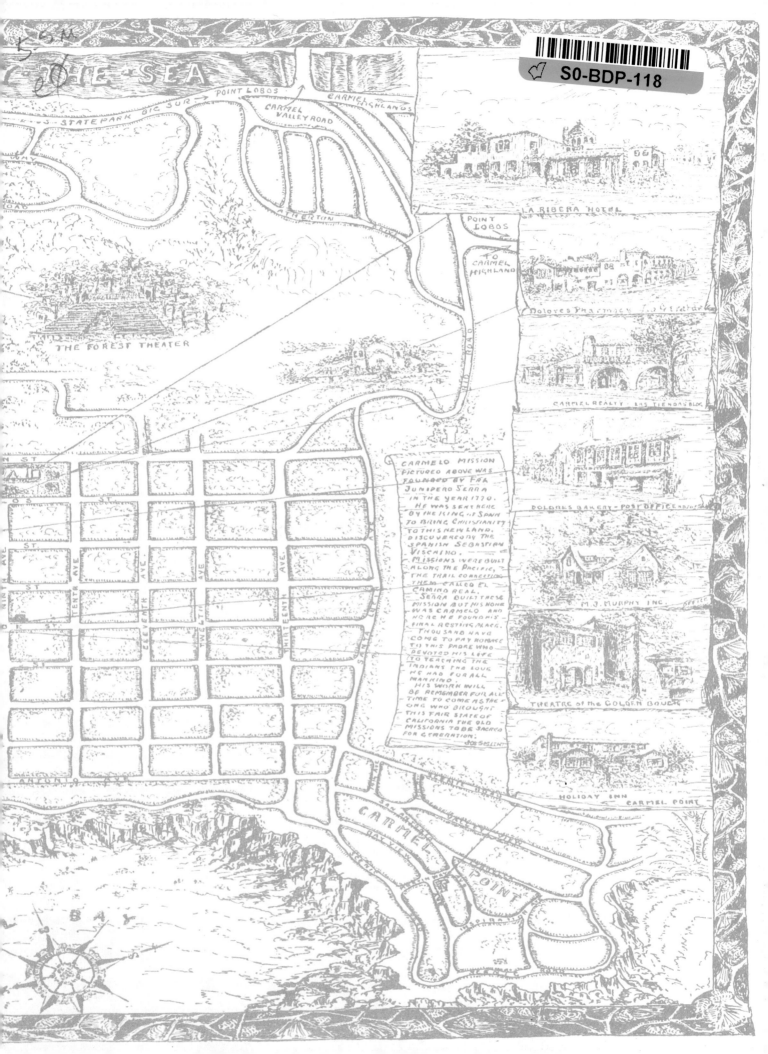

THE SEA

S. STATE PARK BIG SUR → POINT LOBOS   CARMEL HIGHLANDS

CARMEL VALLEY ROAD

ATHERTON

THE FOREST THEATER

POINT LOBOS

TO CARMEL HIGHLAND

LA RIBERA HOTEL

Dolores Pharmacy

CARMEL REALTY · LAS TIENDAS BLDG.

CARMELO MISSION
PICTURED ABOVE WAS
FOUNDED BY FRA
JUNIPERO SERRA
IN THE YEAR 1770.
HE WAS SENT HERE
BY THE KING OF SPAIN
TO BRING CHRISTIANITY
TO THIS NEW LAND.
DISCOVERED BY THE
SPANISH SEBASTIAN
VISCAINO.
MISSIONS WERE BUILT
ALONG THE PACIFIC,
THE TRAIL CONNECTING
THEM CALLED EL
CAMINO REAL.
SERRA BUILT THESE
MISSION BUT HIS HOME
WAS CARMELO AND
HERE HE FOUND HIS
FINAL RESTING PLACE.
THOUSAND HAVE
COME TO PAY HOMAGE
TO THIS PADRE WHO
DEVOTED HIS LIFE
TO TEACHING THE
INDIANS THE LOVE
HE HAD FOR ALL
MANKIND.
HIS WORTH WILL
BE REMEMBER FOR ALL
TIME TO COME AS THE
ONE WHO BROUGHT
THIS FAIR STATE OF
CALIFORNIA THE OLD
MISSIONS TO BE SACRED
FOR GENERATION.

DOLORES BAKERY · POST OFFICE

M. J. MURPHY INC.

THEATRE OF THE GOLDEN BOUGH

NINTH AVE   TENTH AVE   ELEVENTH AVE   TWELFTH AVE   THIRTEENTH AVE   SANTA LUCIA

ANTONIO AVE

HOLIDAY INN   CARMEL POINT

CARMEL   POINT

CARMEL BAY VIEW

BAY

Crème de Carmel

Coastline south of Carmel. Courtesy of the photographer, Kathleen Olson.

Crème de Carmel

The Story of the Lively Personalities
Who Shaped California's Coastal Kingdom

by Donna Marek

ROBERTS RINEHART PUBLISHERS

To my mother, Beverly,
and to Those Who Know.

Contents

Contents

Preface

Carmel, California is revered and awed throughout the world for its beauty, a place to remember. From the time Carmel's rich heritage began with the first Native American inhabitants to the explorers, missionaries and those who have followed, people have developed a passion for this place by the sea which is not easily overcome. From movie stars to ranchers, teachers, artists and marine biologists, people make Carmel the special place it is today.

I, too, have a great fondness for this area which has provided me with extraordinary experiences as a resident over the years. I want to share Carmel's entertaining story of the people, their lifestyles, and the political controversies which have made Carmel the place so many of us have called home. It is my intention in writing this book to give the reader a behind-the-scenes look at Carmel with its outstanding villas and ranches with larkspur-covered hills.

Carmel is a unique blend of population, ethnic heritage, architecture, natural environment, social activities, golf, and abundant wildlife. These topics will also be discussed in this book.

To most people, the word *Carmel* means the entire central coast of California. The town of Carmel By The Sea is located about 130 miles south of San Francisco on Carmel Bay at the southern portion of Monterey Bay on the Monterey Peninsula, 340 miles north of Los Angeles. The town and its narrow and winding tree-lined streets have provided a place sought by artists, writers and celebrities who desired an unconventional lifestyle in an idyllic setting.

The town's neighbors include the unincorporated area directly to the north known as Pebble Beach, a golfer's paradise and home to the 17 Mile Drive; Monterey, California's historic first capitol; Pacific Grove, known as "Butterfly Town U.S.A.;" the outlying eastern area of Salinas, an agricultural center; Carmel Valley, with its rolling hills and ranchland; Big Sur along the rugged coastline to the south; Seaside and Marina, dominated by the military; and the small cities of Del Rey Oaks and Sand City. All of these areas are distinct among themselves, but they are linked by tourism, the economy, politics, the environment and the common need for water.

Carmel lies along the Pacific Ocean and encompasses one of the most dramatic landscapes and meetings of land, sea, and coastal mountains. The area was formed about 40 million years ago during the latter part of the Oligocene period. Monterey

Bay was already in existence at that time as evidenced by marine sediments found in the Monterey and Carmel Bay submarine canyons.

Through various movements of the earth's crust or plates, evidenced by the fault lines found in those canyons and the area's two major faults—the Palo Colorado-San Gregorio and the Monterey Bay fault zones—the area has been subject to tumultuous upheaval. Lava ash found at the shoreline documents volcanic activity. Sea level in Carmel was subject to fluctuations brought about by glaciers melting during the Ice Age.

Some geologists theorize that Carmel and perhaps the entire Monterey Peninsula may have been a passageway to the sea surrounded by a series of islands. Near the Carmel Mission, in portions of Carmel Valley, south near San Simeon and to the east, sedimentary marine deposits called the Monterey Formation give credence to the theory that the Santa Lucia Mountain range along the Big Sur coast was actually an island. This is what explorer Sebastian Vizcaino originally guessed when he discovered Carmel in 1602. The Gabilan Range in the Salinas Valley is also surrounded by these deposits as well as those found to the north at the Santa Cruz Range.

Carmel's climate is moderate with an average high of about 62 degrees Farenheit to a low hovering around 47, although snow has fallen and temperatures have soared into the 90s on rare occasions. The average rainfall is about 18 inches. More rain falls during the months of November through April than at any other time of the year. An average of 183 days are foggy, mostly during the summer months because of changes in current from the Pacific Ocean.

Tourism and the military are the two largest economic bases on the Peninsula. Cultural activities include symphony performances, more than 100 art galleries (about 70 in Carmel-by-the-Sea alone), special events, festivals and places of interest like the Carmel Mission and Fisherman's Wharf.

The Carmel mystique surpasses time. This book takes you on an inside journey to show why Carmel continues to be a special place to those of us who have lived there.

I
Beginnings

The sounds of chanting and music accompanied rhythmic tides along Carmel Beach long before explorers discovered the area.

THE FIRST RESIDENTS

Native Americans, thought to be of Asian descent, first occupied California more than 10,000 years ago. At the time of the first Spanish settlement in 1769, nearly 310,000 Indians lived in California, about 18,000 of them on the central coast. Carmel belonged to the Indians.

Three groups of Native Americans inhabited the Carmel area: the Costanoans, or Ohlones; the Esselens; and the Salinans. The Ohlones lived along the coast of Carmel and Pebble Beach and the inland areas of Carmel Valley. Their population numbered about 7,000. The Esselens, a much smaller group that was centered around Point Sur along the Big Sur coast and in the upper Carmel River areas, were the first to become extinct. The Salinans occupied the Salinas Valley, east of Monterey.

The Ohlones were hunters and gatherers who lived simple and peaceful lives. They worshipped the sun, wore no clothing, and honored a creation myth that included reverence to the eagle, coyote, and hummingbird. Face painting was common, but for some reason the color red was never used. Accounts of the Ohlones' physical appearance describe them as having the very dark skin of Africans, and being of medium height and build, with broad faces and bushy eyebrows similar to Australian Aboriginies.

Abundant shellfish such as crabs, abalone and oysters were gathered at the ocean shore by the Ohlones, and carried in nets or baskets to nearby villages of about 300 inhabitants. Theirs were closely knit communities where elder members of the villages were highly respected. The average life expectancy was about 40 years.

The Indians lived from one harvest to another, and because of the plentiful food supplies they never moved away. Depending upon the season, the Ohlone Indians wandered to the hills to collect acorns, which they ground into flour, or to the Carmel River for salmon. Cormorant chicks were considered delicacies. Beached whales also provided food and the occasion became time for celebration.

The Indians danced, played games and enjoyed Carmel's beautiful shore. Unlike other Indian tribes, the Ohlones didn't collect beadwork. It was too heavy to carry when traveling from the sea to

Costanoan Indian with bow and arrow. Sketch by T. Suria, 1791.

their inland villages. They judged one another and others on their generosity. They believed giving, not having, was wealth.

The Ohlones were advanced in many ways. Evidence from the skulls found at historical sites called middens show that they practiced trepanning, a surgical method of relieving brain tumors. They set broken bones and used herbs for medicines. For serious illness, Shamans were summoned · for spiritual help deeply rooted in the power of their animal gods.

Tobacco and the lime from sea shells were mixed and smoked from stone pipes. These pipes, as well as shell mounds 30 feet deep and other artifacts, have been found at numerous sites around Carmel, at the mouth of the Carmel River, and in Pacific Grove. Artifacts have also been discovered in Pebble Beach near Cypress Point Club, and on Fan Shell Beach at Pescadero Point by private citizens excavating for their homes, and during recon-

struction of a small portion of the Pebble Beach Golf Course.

In the 1970s, the historic sites were monitored by Ohlone Indian descendants such as Patrick Orozco, who worked closely with the California Department of Transportation during excavation.

Many artifacts have been discovered at nearby Point Lobos State Reserve, directly south of Carmel. The Whalers Cove cottage, believed built by Chinese fishermen in the 1850s, displays the artifacts and is open to the public. Point Lobos is filled with the history of several ethnic groups including Chinese and Japanese fishermen, Portuguese whalers and Native Americans. Point Lobos was also the site of a World War II army barracks, a dairy, and an abalone cannery.

When the lost Indian village of Ichxenta was found on the Carmel Bay shores in 1855, an irrigation system and whaling station with a 40' x 40' bar were also discovered. In 1968, Isabelle Meadows, the last known Native American to have spoken the Ohlone language, said the site was a place where grizzly bears ate the whales' remains. It was she who gave the United States government a complete translation of the Costanoan language.

In 1770 many innocent Indians would come from Ichxenta to become part of the mission life. It was a life that changed them and Carmel forever.

THE EXPLORERS

Years before Sebastian Vizcaino sailed into Monterey Bay, Juan Rodriguez Cabrillo and a fleet of thirteen ships sailed northward toward Alta California in 1542. Through a series of mishaps, tortu-

Whale skeleton from a 1901 photograph. The discovery of whale carcasses was a time of celebration for the Ohlones. Courtesy of the Pat Hathaway Collection.

ous weather and illness, the fleet reached only as far as Point Pinos, and narrowly missed discovering Monterey Bay just to the north and literally around the corner. Monterey and Carmel Bays were as elusive then as they are today. Because of their locations off Highway One, the coastal cities of Monterey, Pebble Beach and Pacific Grove can still easily be missed by travelers.

Another 50 years passed before the California coast was explored again, and only after Spain needed ports in which to repair its ships. Pirates and privateers such as Francis Drake attacked Spanish treasure-laden ships on many occasions.

Drake acted on his rights as an Englishman to claim land east of Carmel for Queen Elizabeth and England because the coastal Indians of the Miwok tribe, who lived farther inland from Carmel, gave up their land voluntarily to him. According to Drake, the Indians had given him title to their land when they gave him a crown after inviting him to address a meeting in their village.

There was some conflict between England and Spain in the taking of land in California. Pope Clement V's order in 1529 gave Spain the right to conquer the Indians and take their land. In 1532, Francisco Vitoria, a teacher at the University of

Pristine Carmel shores greeted European explorers. Courtesy of the Pat Hathaway Collection.

Salamanca in Spain, said that Spain's claims were only good on unoccupied land. He said occupied land belonged to the original inhabitants, namely the Indians.

England viewed the issue differently. The English government observed that only *occupied* land could be claimed and that Pope Clement V had no right to claim anything. Spain was moved to respond to this open taking of the land by England.

In 1596, Spain's Viceroy Luis de Valesco gave Sebastian Vizcaino, a successful Spanish merchant engaged in pearl fishing, permission to explore the California coast. He was instructed to avoid conflicts with the Indians and ordered not to sail into the Gulf of Mexico. Vizcaino departed from Acapulco, Mexico on May 5, 1602 with a company of soldiers, their wives, horses, an expert map mak-er, Geronimo Martinez de Palarjos, and three Carmelite friars on board his ship the *San Diego*.

While sailing northward, Vizcaino discovered a mountain range off the Big Sur Coast that he named the Santa Lucia Mountains. In front of them to the north was a white-sand beach with a vast stretch of natural beauty. At first, he thought he had discovered an island. On December 16, 1602, he discovered a large bay and named it Monterey Bay after the Mexican viceroy, the Count of Monterey.

Vizcaino and his men spent three weeks exploring the area. They discovered the Carmel River and named it El Rio Carmello, after the Carmelite friars. They named the land Carmel after Mount Carmel in the Holy Land where the Carmelite Order was founded.

These three Jo Mora illustrations from Hotel Del Monte menus of 1936 depict the Spanish exploration and conquest of the Monterey area. From left to right: pirates besiege the Viceroy of Mexico's galleon; Vizcaino comes ashore at Monterey Bay in 1602; Father Serra reclaims California for Spain in 1770. Courtesy of the Pebble Beach Company.

In a letter to the viceroy written on December 28, 1602, eighteen years before the Pilgrims landed at Plymouth Rock, Vizcaino described the flowers; the oak and pine trees which could be used for ship building; the temperate climate; and the plentiful fish and fowl. He called the elusive Monterey Bay a "noble harbor" that was well protected from the elements.

In his letter he said, "I advise His Majesty concerning the great extent of this land and its numerous population and what promise it holds forth, and what the Indians have given me to understand concerning the people of the interior, and of how gentle and affable the people are so that they will receive readily, as I think, the holy gospel and will come into subjection to the royal crown . . ."

The Carmelite friars said mass at a huge oak tree near the shore. The tree became known as the Vizcaino Oak and there are various stories about the tree, including one that tells how it was damaged by lightning and chopped down by a work crew in 1905. Supposedly, fishermen retrieved the tree and a monument marks its location at Fisherman's Wharf in Monterey.

By the time Vizcaino returned to Spain, a new viceroy had been named. The Marquis de Monte-sclaros received Vizcaino's enthusiastic report, but the viceroy had other plans which didn't include Monterey or Carmel.

In the meantime, England, France, Holland and Russia were very interested in claiming land in North America. In 1745, the Russians reached the Aleutian Islands and their fur trading and commer-cial-fishing establishments were moving southward toward California. A Franciscan monk, Mariano Martinez, reported to Spain that the Russians were quickly moving toward Monterey. Spain began a movement to develop the California missions years before Napoleon's invasion of Moscow in June of 1812, which stopped the Russian advance.

Father Junipero Serra, founder of the California missions. Courtesy of the Local History Department, Harrison Memorial Library.

THE MISSION LIFE

The Franciscan priest Father Junipero Serra is credited with establishing the mission system in California. Serra was born in Petra on the Isle of Mallorca, Spain in 1713 and was baptized Michael Joseph. He took the name of Junipero when he was ordained as a Franciscan priest. St. Francis of Assisi, who founded that order in 1209, had a diminutive-sized companion named Junipero. Father Serra himself was only five feet, three inches tall.

In 1963, Carmel's mayor, Eben Whittlesey, signed a resolution making Petra Carmel's sister city, a designation that holds today.

In 1749, Serra was selected to become a mis-sionary in Mexico City along with his two close friends, Father Francisco Palou and Father Juan Crespi. Both had been Serra's students when he was a professor at the Royal Monastery of San Francisco in Palma, Spain.

Although Serra received a dispensation to travel the 270–mile distance by mule from the port of Vera Cruz to Mexico City, Serra chose to walk. During this arduous journey, Serra was bitten in the leg by a poisonous insect and developed an in-fection. Because of this incident, Serra endured a serious limp for the rest of his life. After two years, Serra became the President of the Sierra Gorda Missions, a position he held for six years until he was recalled to Mexico City.

For ten years Serra was in Mexico City, a place he came to loathe because of the over-indulgent lifestyles of the wealthy Spaniards while he knew poor people went hungry. He enjoyed the time he spent in areas outside of Mexico City where he could help the Indians and farmers. Father Palou traveled with Serra on these journeys which, over a period of seven years, were estimated to be around 2,000 miles. Serra lived a very austere life, slept little and prayed more than anything else. In an act which appears to have been one of self-punishment, he is said to have worn clothing woven with barbed wire!

It was in 1767 that Serra received the news that he should return to Mexico City to begin the biggest challenge to his proven leadership abilities. In 1768 the king of Spain, Charles III, selected General Jose de Galvez and Father Junipero Serra to oversee the Jesuit-run missions in Baja California. The Jesuits, or Black Friars, became unpopular with Europeans and Charles III, who wanted to replace them with Franciscan priests. General Galvez had risen through the ranks after marrying an influential Frenchwoman.

During this period, Baja California—which consisted of the northern half of the lower California peninsula—was considered a state of Mexico. Alta California was the area north of San Diego toward San Francisco.

Galvez directed the immense expedition which consisted of three ships and two land contingents. Father Crespi traveled by land under the direction of Captain Fernando Rivera y Moncada along with nearly fifty Christian Indians. Father Serra traveled in the second land contingent with the governor of Baja California, Gaspar de Portola. Two weeks after reaching San Diego, Portola continued the land journey with Father Crespi. Father Serra stayed in San Diego where he established the first California mission, San Diego de Alcalá. The Kings Highway, or El Camino Real, began there and eventually led to the twenty-one missions that extended from San Diego to Sonoma.

Portola and Crespi continued northward near what is now Highway One through the nearly impassable Santa Lucia Mountains of Big Sur. From a hilltop Portola saw a small bay and river which he didn't realize was the Carmel River or Carmel and Monterey Bays, previously discovered by Vizcaino. The party erected a cross at Monterey Bay and left letters about their travels in the soil. They continued to San Francisco and later returned south to San Diego.

In 1770, Father Serra accompanied Portola on a journey north where they came upon Carmel and Monterey Bays. To their surprise, the cross Portola erected on his previous journey was surrounded by Indian artifacts. The Indians honored the cross, fearing that if they didn't, they might anger the spirits of the only white men they had seen who wore crosses. Portola uncovered the letters buried the previous year. A mass was said at the same site where explorer Vizcaino and the Carmelite friars had said mass nearly 150 years earlier.

King Charles III had given Portola and Serra the responsibilities of erecting a mission at Monterey, establishing a presidio, or military base, to enforce and protect the area from invaders, and of coloniz-

The Carmel Mission was founded on June 30, 1770. Father Serra is buried beneath the altar there. Courtesy of the Diocese of Monterey.

ing the Indians through Christianity. After establishing the missions, the Spanish government would follow Pope Clement V's order and adeptly use the mission system to peacefully control the Indian population and rid the land of the Indians at the same time.

On June 3, 1770, Serra began the San Carlos de Monterey Mission in Monterey. One year later, believing that the Presidio soldiers would have a negative effect on the Indians, Serra moved the mission to the Carmel River on Carmel Bay where he could take advantage of better agricultural conditions for the Indians. It was renamed the Mission San Carlos de Borremeo, or what is now simply known as the Carmel Mission.

The original mission in Monterey was the Presidio Chapel, which became the San Carlos Cathedral in Monterey. It has a courtyard which was used as the site of the marriage of Herbert Hoover and Lou Henry. The chapel is now known as the Royal Presidio Chapel.

In 1771, the Carmel Mission was bounded by the Pacific Ocean on the west, the Santa Lucia Mountains on the south, the Gabilan Mountain Range to the east, and open ranch land to the north. Log buildings with flat roofs were built on the mission site by Indian labor. The first buildings were a chapel, a kitchen, a house, and granary. Plantings came from Mexico, and wildflowers covered much of the surrounding lands.

One of the Indians who helped build the mission was Juan Onesimo. The mission priests gave him a violin which he considered a prized possession. His descendants lived in Carmel Valley for many years.

The peaceful, innocent, and curious Indians independently went to the Mission to learn about Christianity. The priests told them Bible stories, fed and baptized them.

By agreement, once the Indians were baptized, they had to remain at the mission and work. The mission priests taught them the European ways of weaving and farming. Fathers Palou and Crespi later joined Serra at the Mission, and reported that Serra made clothing for the Indians and generally cared for them. Serra taught them to salute and say the words "love to God."

The Indians' sexual promiscuity was thwarted by the priests, who soon separated the men and women unless they were married. The precise records kept by the priests reveal that there were more marriages and baptisms in 1774 at the Carmel Mission than at any of the other missions in California.

Old Gabriel, the first Indian baptized at the Mission, later helped build the Soledad and San Gabriel Missions. It is estimated that he was at least 120 years of age, making him the oldest human being in the world at the time of his death in 1890. He was buried at the Carmel Mission Cemetery along with thousands of other Indians.

There are conflicting interpretations about the Indians' mission lives, however. During the mission period (1770–1834), the Indians lost their land, their culture, and their freedom. Many believe the Indians were doomed as soon as the mission was established. The once disease-free Indian popula-

Descendants of Onesimo, an Indian who helped build the Carmel Mission. Courtesy of the Mayo Hays Library.

tion suffered at the overcrowded missions where they were exposed to western diseases. As time went by the soldiers no longer strictly enforced the baptism agreement. When the Indians ran away, many times the soldiers did not return them to the missions. This upset Father Serra.

Even when historian Jean Francois Galoup de la Perouse arrived in 1786, the Indians lived in squalor. He observed that when the soldiers returned the Indians to the missions, they were punished by whipping. Punishment was chosen by a missionary priest in the same manner that an overseer might treat a slave.

Perouse, a follower of Voltaire and supporter of the Enlightment, came with an elaborate and well-outfitted French expedition of two ships with physicians, famous scientists and cartographers. He was commissioned by King Louis XVI to observe and gather scientific data about areas along the Pacific Ocean and California coast. He spent ten days at the Carmel Mission and observed how the Indians were placed in stocks like prisoners.

As years went by there were fewer converts to Christianity, and more Indians ran away. Father Serra, who had been in failing health, died at the mission on August 28, 1784.

After the collapse of the mission system in the 1800s, the Ohlone Indians disbanded and disappeared completely, although a few of them tried unsuccessfully to restore their villages. The last known tribal dance was held in 1897.

In 1808, Spain's ships were being attacked by pirates and supplies to California were slow in arriving. Between 1808-1820s, there was massive discontent with Spain's 300-year-rule over the area.

A Carmel Valley oak tree displays a cross carved by Indians. Courtesy of the Mayo Hays Library.

In November 1818, two ships, the *Argentina*, under the command of a revolutionary French pirate named Hippolyte de Bouchard, and the *Santa Rosa*, commanded by Peter Corney, invaded Monterey Bay. The *Santa Rosa* fired on the presidio and Bouchard sent a letter ahead asking for Monterey's surrender. The last of California's Spanish governors, Pablo Sola, retaliated but proved to be no match for the army of men from the two ships. Although boats were launched off Point Pinos, Sola quickly retreated to Salinas. Days later, soldiers, residents and Indians from the east county areas banded together under Sola with the determination to take back Monterey. When they arrived, however, Monterey had been looted and abandoned by the invaders.

Mexico's War for Independence from Spanish rule was complicated and lengthy, with many battles fought throughout Spain's various colonial provinces. On September 27, 1821, the last Spanish viceroy of Mexico, Juan de O'Donoju, signed the Treaty of Cordova, which acknowledged that Mexico had won the war and its independence from Spain.

In 1833, under Governor Jose Maria Echeandia, the mission lands which provided the region with an economic base were secularized. Control was taken from the church and the Franciscan order and given to civilians who would be politically supportive of the governor. Originally, the California missions were supposed to be changed into civilian towns after a ten-year period, but this never occurred. The mission lands were completely sold. The first large Mexican land grant was ordered by Juan Bautista Alvardo, the first native Mexican governor. It was called Rancho el Pescadero, awarded to Fabian Barreto, and included Carmel and Pebble Beach.

Because the government stopped financially supporting the missions, they eventually went to ruin. The roof collapsed at the Carmel Mission in 1852. In the 1870s, Reverend Angelo Cassanova began an effort to save the Carmel Mission, but it wasn't until the 1950s that Sir Harry Downie, an expert at mission renovation, began the actual project of bringing the Carmel Mission back to life. In fact, it was Downie who found the original cross set by Father Serra in 1771 at the mission.

Evidence of Father Serra's influence abounds in Carmel. A statue at the corner of San Carlos and Second Streets is a familiar sight for visitors finding their way into town, and Junipero Street is named after him. In 1924 Carmel sculptor Jo Mora honored Serra with a sarcophagus, a stone coffin, which lies in the mission Basilica. Fathers Serra, Crespi and Palou are buried under the Basilica in front of the altar. A mosaic mural of Serra was placed on the side of the Carmel Plaza Shopping Center on Ocean Avenue. Poet George Sterling even wrote a poem about him. In 1937 the Roman Catholic Church began a movement to grant Serra sainthood because of his leadership in developing the California missions. A final decision is still pending.

Father Serra statue at the corner of San Carlos and Second Streets. Courtesy of the Local History Department, Harrison Memorial Library.

The Pope's Visit

On Thursday, September 17, 1987, Pope John Paul II honored Carmel and Father Junipero Serra by visiting the Carmel Mission. Carmel city council members and about 500 people fortunate to receive tickets saw the Pope at the Basilica.

The Pope was greeted by several public officials including Monterey Mayor Dan Albert, United States Congressman Leon Panetta, State Senator Henry Mello, Rear Admiral Robert Austin, Superintendent of the Naval Post Graduate School, Carmel Mayor Clint Eastwood (who stood 13th in line), and State Representative Eric Seastrand. Bishop Thadeus Shubsda told the Pope that Seastrand was battling cancer, and the Pope told Seastrand they would battle together. With photographers everywhere, the Pope broke from the line and personally greeted the honored Fourth Degree Knights of Columbus, which represents the highest degree of that Catholic fraternal organization for men.

While waiting for the Pope's plane to land at the Monterey Airport, Mayor Clint Eastwood told members of the media that the Pontiff was also an actor, referring to the Pope's early studies for the stage.

The Pope's visit brought Serra's beatification process closer to becoming reality. In September of 1988, Serra was beatified by the Roman Catholic Church, one step from canonization or sainthood. Eighteen cloistered nuns from the nearby Carmelite Monastery were permitted to visit with the Pope as he prayed at the mission.

Later in the day, Pope John Paul II said mass at Laguna Seca raceway, located midway between Monterey and Salinas. The raceway had been changed to accommodate the event. Thousands of flowers surrounded the altar. About 100,000 people, many from out of state, were bused from various locations to hear the historic mass. This peaceful and inspiring day was not without controversy, however.

Che Quesch Auh-Ho-Oh, a Chumash Indian from Pacific Grove, led a group of Indians who began a prayer vigil at the Mission on Monday, a few days before the Pope's anticipated visit. They wanted to hold a forty-eight-hour prayer vigil at the Carmel Mission in honor of their an-

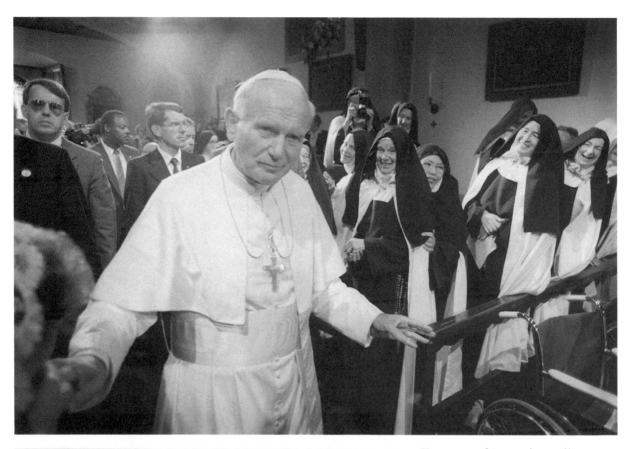

Two views of Pope John Paul's 1987 visit to Carmel. Above: nuns express joy at meeting the Pope at the Carmel Mission on September 17, 1987. Courtesy of Jim Gensheimer, *San Jose Mercury News*. At left: Costanoan tribal chief Anthony Miranda and Che Quesch Auh-Ho-Oh attempt to hold a prayer vigil outside the Carmel Mission gates. The Monterey County Sheriff's Department interceded and stopped the vigil, claiming the small group required a permit. Courtesy of the *Monterey Peninsula Herald*.

cestors who built and lived at the original mission. The Monterey County Sheriff's Department interceded and stopped the vigil, explaining that the small group of Indians needed a permit. The descendants of the Costanoan Indians were thus denied access to the Carmel Mission.

The Indians appealed to the Monterey County Supervisors, who officially refused their request on many technicalities, saying the application was too late to hold public hearings on the issue. Upon learning of this decision, Bishop Thaddeus Shubsda, head of the Monterey Diocese of Catholic Churches, affirmed the Supervisors' decision and also denied the Indians access to the Mission. Several Indians did stand at the corner of Highway One and Rio Road with signs proclaiming Native American rights, however.

Following the Pope's visit, the area was left in turmoil. Many people were stranded at Laguna Seca when buses broke down or simply never arrived; the County of Monterey later sued the bus companies for abandoning the visitors. The Diocese of Monterey incurred a $1 million debt because of the expenses involved in providing security, and staging the mass itself. In addition, some scholars and theologians expressed disappointment because the Pope had not addressed key issues such as birth control.

It took many months before the Peninsula returned to its normal complacency, with only the memory of that extraordinary visit lingering in the minds of residents.

II
The Early Years

Monterey thrived as California's first capitol, leaving Carmel virtually forgotten until the late 1880s. Except for the Carmel Mission, nearby Mexican ranchos, and the Mission Ranch, the area was undeveloped.

The Mission's nearest neighbor was the Mission Ranch, owned by William Martin, one of many people from Scotland who originally came to California for gold. On the other side of the Mission lay property owned by a Frenchman, a rancher and baker named Honore Escolle. His property included a hilly and forested area called "Las Manzanitas" after the plants that grew there.

CARMEL CITY

In 1888, Monterey developer Santiago J. Duckworth purchased Escolle's Manzanitas property, where he built his own cottage at what is now Carpenter and Second Streets, north of Ocean Avenue in the tree-lined hills now known as Carmel Woods. Duckworth surveyed the 80-acre tract and sold lots for $20.00 each to anyone who would promise to build on them.

Duckworth printed brochures advertising his development as a Catholic community called "Carmel City" because of its proximity to the Mission.

In reality, the Mission was two miles away and badly in need of repair.

Monterey priest Father Antonio Cassanova and Mrs. Leland Stanford of San Francisco, the wealthy wife of a railroad baron, started a fundraising drive for the Mission, and David Starr Jordan, Stanford University's first president, wrote about Carmel's beauty in an 1888 *Scribners* magazine article. All of this attention to the area neatly played into Duckworth's plans to develop Carmel. So many professors from the San Francisco area began purchasing property in Carmel that one section of town on Camino Real became known as Professors Row.

Duckworth even built a glass–walled bathhouse on Carmel Beach hoping to lure visitors, and a hotel for potential buyers of his lots.

At the same time, however, the elaborate Hotel Del Monte in Monterey with its Roman baths and swank dining hall was drawing wealthy guests from all over the country. The Southern Pacific Railroad traveled only as far as Monterey but not near Carmel, so that by the late 1890s interest in Carmel began to decline. Land began selling for only a few dollars per lot. The economy lapsed and tourist competition from Monterey's hotel became too much for "Carmel City." Carmel never became

So many professors from the San Francisco area moved to Carmel that Camino Real Street was also known as Professors Row. This cottage was located at 7th and Camino Real. Courtesy of the Local History Department, Harrison Memorial Library.

the large Catholic enclave that Duckworth envisioned, but before long two other businessmen picked up where Duckworth left off.

THE TOWN

In 1902, James Franklin Devendorf, the largest San Jose area landholder at the time and his partner, San Francisco attorney Frank Powers, purchased the Carmel City land from Duckworth and added other parcels as well. They formed the Carmel Development Company and earned the

reputation as Carmel's co-founders. Under their development the town became known as Carmel-by-the-Sea in 1903.

They divided Ocean Avenue, which has become the town's main street, into north and south directions. The dirt street was either very dry and filled with potholes, or looked like a stream running toward the ocean during the rainy season.

Duckworth's hotel was moved on rollers to the current location of the Pine Inn. Monterey Pine

Early visitors sit beneath the large Carmel bathhouse built by Santiago Duckworth in the 1880s. Courtesy of the Pat Hathaway Collection.

trees were planted along Ocean Avenue in 1904, trees that would eventually cause major conflicts to residents later in the century when residents wanted to remove them for various reasons.

Within a year, the town began to thrive and more than thirty families moved to Carmel. L. S. Slevin started the post office and a stationery store; restaurants and a stable were built. The Sunset School opened in a cottage on Dolores Street. It was later moved to Devendorf Park, and eventually to 9th and San Carlos Streets, the site of the Sunset Center. The town was on its way to becoming a complete seaside community. Carmel began at-

tracting artists, writers and actors from the San Francisco area.

The quaint seaside town of Carmel became a place where dogs had their owners' names and mail was picked up at the post office. (Houses didn't have numbers but had names instead, a tradition carried through to this day. In order to have mail delivered to homes in Carmel, sidewalks and curbs would be necessary and Carmel doesn't have either in the residential areas.) A bulletin board adjacent to the post office made the area a social gathering place where residents also posted ads and shared gossip. Milk shrines, which were located in

George Bellows, Sutton Palmer, Matteo Sandona, and David Lester Boronda were some of the local resident artists who attended club meetings. Boronda, who was born on a Salinas Valley cattle ranch, had a great grandfather who was the area's first grizzly bear hunter. The Boronda home is now occupied by the Monterey County Historical Society. In the late 1920s, the Carmel Artists Association was formed by a group of nineteen local and

Franklin Devendorf and family, from a 1916 photo. Devendorf and his partner, Frank Powers, are credited with the founding of Carmel. Courtesy of the Pat Hathaway Collection.

In 1924 residents picked up their fresh milk at "milk shrines" located throughout Carmel. Courtesy of the Local History Department, Harrison Memorial Library.

various areas throughout the town, also created another way for residents to meet: here they picked up their daily orders of fresh, bottled milk in compartments that resembled book shelves.

In 1903, Frank Powers built the first artist's studio in Carmel for his wife, Jane. It was at the north end of Carmel in a grove of eucalyptus trees, near the Carmel gate into Pebble Beach. A second studio was built of redwood and stone for artist Jessie Francis Short.

In 1905 the Carmel Arts and Crafts Club was organized by Elsie Allen. It provided a gallery for artists in return for thirty percent of any profits.

A bulletin board next to the post office was the place for exchanging gossip and posting ads. Courtesy of the Local History Department, Harrision Memorial Library.

legendary artists.

In 1905, James Franklin Devendorf donated two lots for Carmel's first church, the Methodist Church of the Wayfarer. Many of Carmel's churches were originally located at the current site of the Pine Inn, including the All Saints Episcopal and the Christian Science Churches. The All Saints Episcopal Church is now located on Dolores and 9th Streets and was the site of one of the 1986 mayoral debates. In the 1950s, the Presbyterian Church was built by the Comstock Associates. (President Dwight D. Eisenhower visited the church on one occasion.) The building later became the Carmel-by-the-Sea City Hall.

Many people began moving to Carmel from San Francisco. Perry Newberry and his wife, Bertha Blair Brubaker, became active in the town and lived on Dolores Street between 12th and 13th Streets. He became editor and publisher of the *Carmel Pine Cone,* and was elected a city trustee on the platform to keep Carmel the same as it always was—a small seaside community.

Herbert Heron Peet founded the Forest Theater in 1910. He was Carmel's first actor-mayor. The theater became a uniting and conflicting place for the entire community when egos became involved and power plays made.

In September 1890 the Hotel Carmelo was the only structure on Ocean Avenue—now Carmel's busy main street. Courtesy of the Pat Hathaway Collection.

When Frank Powers initiated the idea of a Carmel library in 1906, he was met with an enthusiastic response from the residents. The Carmel Development Company donated a building and volunteers formed the staff. Twenty years later, Ella Reid Harrison donated the funds for a new building which became the Harrison Memorial Library, named after her husband, the California State Supreme Court Justice Ralph Chandler Harrison. Architect Bernard Maybeck designed the library of wood and stone in a Spanish and Mediterranean style. The structure was built by Carmel's master builder, M. J. Murphy. Today, a new Park Branch includes Carmel's History Room. The library currently serves nearly 20,000 residents of the area, including those from Pebble Beach.

Along with the town's many other shops, there was a forge where horseshoes and other metal objects were made. Francis Whittaker, a popular resident, was considered to be the county's black-smith expert and metal artist. He was a colorful personality who on one occasion threw himself in front of a bulldozer on the beach and challenged the driver to move it! His Carmel blacksmith shop later became the site of a popular restaurant called The Forge in the Forest.

A stable was located at Junipero and Fifth Streets. Architect Charles Sumner Greene's daughter-in-law, Bette Greene, married to Gordon Greene, ran the stable.

Bluett's Ice Cream Parlor, a gathering-place for locals on Ocean Avenue, is now the Dick Bruen Building. The store's basement contained a firing range and boxing ring run by the chief of police.

The Leidig Brothers Market on Ocean Avenue was run by the family until 1915. Carmel's longest-living resident, Glenn Leidig, was born on January 31, 1912. He and his wife, Marian, reside on the same land where he grew up as a boy in Carmel. Glenn Leidig recalled that his family originally lived in Salinas and knew the Steinbeck family. The Leidigs' Salinas home is now on the National Register of Historic Places. Some members of the family were pony express riders. He said his family also had a lumberyard in Carmel, where the current Nielsen's Market is located on San Carlos and Seventh Street.

The Tortilla Flats area was located at Guadalupe and Mission Streets from about 1928-1930. It was considered a shantytown by many people, although it wasn't a poverty-stricken area. Leidig said the Flats area was a place where affordable housing was available to workers from the family's lumberyard.

Ocean Avenue and San Carlos Street, looking east. The Carmel drugstore was a popular source of liquor during Prohibition. Courtesy of the Local History Department, Harrison Memorial Library.

In 1909, resident Sinclair Lewis dressed in a Dutch maid's costume to promote the annual Dutch Market, an event where artists and business people worked together to raise funds for the Arts and Crafts Club.

Since 1915, a water shortage problem has existed in Carmel. James Franklin Devendorf occasionally trucked in water for the town. Electricity came to Carmel in 1915, and the *Carmel Pine Cone* began publication.

On October 31, 1916, Carmel officially became a town, an event that is marked every year by a Halloween parade. Carmel's first mayor was A.P. Fraser who served from 1916–1920. There were no building restrictions at that time. Deals were made to attract buyers and bring people to Carmel, not keep them away. The first city codes established that livestock could not run free through town, and the second protected trees.

In the 1920s, when a group of investors proposed to build a large Spanish style hotel at the

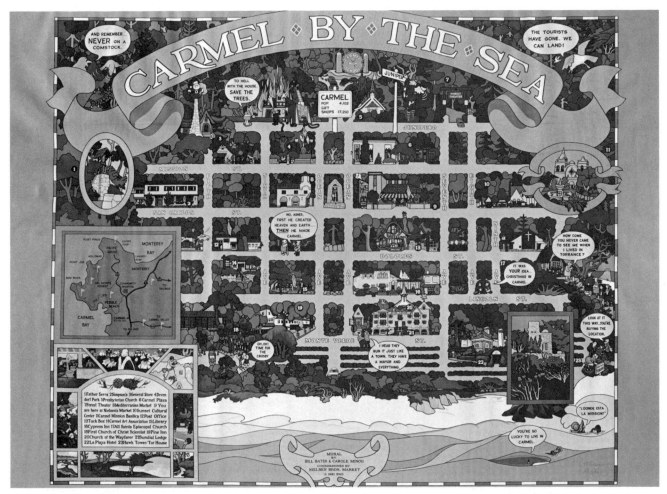

Nielson Brothers Market commissioned this humorous map of Carmel to commemorate the town's 70th birthday in 1986. Artists Bill Bates and Carol Minou painted the map, which is located outside the market on San Carlos Street. Courtesy of Merv and Nanci Sutton.

bottom of Ocean Avenue, the artists protested and for the first time the town was divided between commercial and resident interests. Prompted by growing tension, Carmel's city council passed an ordinance in 1929 called the Magna Carta which set the record straight. It stated that Carmel's residential interests take high priority over commercial ones. In other words, if there was a conflict over any issue which puts commercial in opposition to residential interests, residential interests must prevail. The Magna Carta is in effect today and is stated on a placard in City Hall. Similar conflicts between commercial and residential interests have continued throughout Carmel's history, becoming a major focus of the 1986 Carmel mayoral campaign.

In 1916, the Carmel-by-the-Sea Chapter of the Red Cross was chartered but it wasn't until World War II that it became active. The Red Cross collected clothing and items which were shipped to hospitals. Later, a substantial amount of knit goods were supplied to veterans' hospitals. From 1937 through 1991, Carmel's Red Cross chapter was the only one in the United States providing free ambulance service to residents. In 1991, however, after a political ballot measure was passed requiring paramedics to man the ambulances, the chapter ceased the service. Now the area is served by the Carmel Regional Ambulance Service.

A 1980 agreement with the Community Hospital of the Monterey Peninsula provided that all blood drawn at bloodmobiles in the area must stay in the same area and be available to local residents.

Carmel began experiencing all the significant problems of a town in conflict over growth. In 1926, Argyll Campbell, Carmel's City Attorney, suggested a wall be built around Carmel to keep it from developing any further. (Pebble Beach had already erected fences around its property and was charging gate fees by this time.) By the mid-1940s, a Planning Commission was established and began dictating sign ordinances. In 1925, an ordinance prohibiting "obnoxious industries" like soap and chemical factories was established. Years later, the town passed a rule which stopped anyone from placing plastic plants outdoors. Carmel wanted to remain authentic in every way.

In 1958, Gunnar Norberg became mayor and was known for his anti-growth stand on issues. When it came time to vote to save Carmel's Sunset Cultural Center, Norberg voted no. Fortunately for the town, the vote went against him but he maintained his stand against progress even into the 1980s.

In 1950 the non-profit Carmel Foundation began assisting elderly, low-income residents in finding housing so they could continue to live in Carmel. In the late 1980s, several buildings were added to the already-established residences owned by the Foundation. To this date, there is always a waiting list and housing is rented on the basis of need.

Carmel's popularity grew as developers contiued to entice San Francisco area residents to live and build in Carmel. As time went by, artists moved to Carmel and their unique personalities and fame provided another lure for visitors and prospective residents.

III

An Artists Colony

Artists never thrive in colonies. Ants do!

The author Henry Miller uttered those words while living in Big Sur. The statement may be true, but Carmel had its very own artists colony for a few years, regardless.

Developer James Franklin Devendorf tried to interest San Francisco artists in moving to Carmel. He offered poet George Ansel Sterling and writer Mary Austin free land if they promised to build in Carmel. Those two writers are credited with starting Carmel's artists colony, which ultimately included many notables.

GEORGE STERLING

In 1901, Sterling and Jack London became friends when they lived in San Francisco and belonged to the Bohemian Club, a haven for journalists since its founding in 1872. Later, when musicians, artists, and actors were allowed membership, the journalists objected and the Press Club was formed. Today, the Bohemian Club is still a haven for very wealthy and powerful members.

Sterling, London and famed trial lawyer, Earl Rogers, socialized together often. They were so drunk on one occcasion that they were all jailed. When they were released, Rogers refused to leave and threatened to sue for false arrest.

Both Sterling and London drank and had active social lives that included numerous brief affairs with several women. London called Sterling "Greek" and Sterling called London "Wolf." When Carrie Sterling finally confronted her husband about his womanizing and drinking, they talked about moving out of San Francisco.

The Sterlings decided to live and farm in Carmel. He called it the "Chosen Land." But instead of escaping from the big-city influences, Sterling found himself in the midst of a new arena. He was a recognized Bohemian poet. Soon his friends Mary Austin and Jack London started to visit. Those early visits were not only an excuse to have multi-day parties and major beach picnics, but became the true beginning of the colony. The artists quickly found out that while prohibition was in full swing, liquor could be bought at the drugstore in Carmel.

At each of the beach parties, Sterling added a verse to a popular local song called the "Abalone Song." Because of those parties a rule was made by the writers which said they were not to be disturbed before noon.

After Ambrose Bierce wrote an article in *Cosmo-*

Poet George Sterling, shown here collecting abalone along the Carmel shore, was considered the founder of Carmel's artists colony. Courtesy of the Pat Hathaway Collection.

Sterling's friend Jack London was a frequent visitor to Carmel. Courtesy of the Pat Hathaway Collection.

politan recognizing Sterling's poetic genius, Carmel gained popularity and Sterling attracted even more guests. Bierce himself had been a friend and a significant influence on Sterling's work for years.

The gifted poet wrote "Titanic Edifice," a dedication to the Golden Gate Bridge which was later read at the bridge's opening in 1937.

Sterling had his own personal idiosyncracies. He gathered abalone, one of his favorite pastimes. He even built a pagan altar surrounded by the skulls of horses and cattle in the forest behind his house on Torres Street.

MARY AUSTIN

Mary Austin was married to Stafford Austin, but lived apart from him in a life of solitude, except for her strong friendship with Sterling. He confided in her about his many affairs. They played like children and acted out their fantasies on the beach. Her novel, *Outland,* was based on their Carmel escapades. Austin was one of the few writers who didn't drink. She surrounded herself with powerful people such as the Herbert Hoover family and Stanford University's president, David Starr Jordan.

Her autobiography, *Earth Horizon,* revealed that she didn't need love affairs to release her subconscious. Austin was considered a forerunner to contemporary feminists because she wrote on women's issues.

Mary Austin (far right) and friends at an early Carmel beach party. Courtesy of the Pat Hathaway Collection.

She described her passion for mystical and spiritual philosophies in her 1913 book *The Green Bough*. Her interests in Native American spiritualism made people talk, and residents found her a bit odd when she pranced around an altar stone near the ocean in a white dress with her long hair flowing. The stone was near what became Robinson Jeffers' Tor House. Eventually people became accustomed to her ways but many called her such unkindly names as the "sacred cow."

She was a prolific and successful author and worked earnestly at her Carmel home in a place she called her "wick-i-up," a treehouse of sorts. When Austin became ill with cancer, she moved to Europe. After a brief stay she miraculously regained her health and credited her spiritualism for her recovery. Upon returning to Carmel she realized it had changed and then moved to Santa Fe, New Mexico, where she was surrounded by people who shared her philosophies.

26

Mary Austin in her wick-i-up, where she wrote many of her books. Courtesy of the Pat Hathaway Collection.

OTHER FRIENDS

James (Jimmy) Marie Hopper was also part of Carmel's colony. After graduating from the University of California Law School, he became a reporter and befriended Sterling and London, the latter of whom described him in his *Valley of the Moon.* Many times Hopper and Sterling dove for abalone together and enjoyed beach parties where they drank wine and beer. Both men lived on Torres Street.

Upton Sinclair came to Carmel at Sterling's invitation. Sinclair had founded Helicon Hall in New Jersey, a gathering place for writers, socialists and spiritualists. After the Hall was destroyed by fire, Sinclair visited Carmel for a few months, but found himself so lethargic that he soon moved to Southern California. He wasn't the only one to feel the ease of the lifestyle; Sterling himself didn't write for four years. The sea coast was a good excuse to do nothing but socialize. Of course, the Costanoan Indians must have realized this as they refreshed and rested at the beach in early history.

Michael Williams and two sisters, Alice Mac-Gowan and Grace MacGowan Cooke, writers who came to Carmel from Helicon Hall, later brought their friend Sinclair Lewis. At one time during his stay in Carmel, Lewis worked as a dishwasher in a local restaurant. Harry Leon Wilson, the author of *The Spenders,* arrived in 1910 and settled in the Carmel Highlands.

So many writers were living in Carmel that the post office placed a container outside the building containing nothing but manuscript rejections received by the writers. In fact, Wilson said there were more rejections at that post office than any other place in the country.

IN THE SHADOWS

Another of Sterling's friends who visited Carmel and also knew Jimmy Hopper was the poet Nora May French. Despite her talent and promise, French cut her own life short with cyanide at the Sterling's home one day. Her ashes were scattered

THE NEWEST MAGNETIZING CENTER.

HOTBED OF SOULFUL CULTURE, VORTEX OF EROTIC ERUDITION.

Carmel in California, Where Author and Artist Folk Are Establishing the Most Amazing Colony on Earth.

BY WILLARD HUNTINGTON WRIGHT.

CARMEL-BY-THE-SEA is a very temperamental town.

Situated five miles from Monterey in a huge pine grove which slopes to the sea, Carmel has been blessed with much natural beauty. Its abundant foliage, lush ravines, picturesque hills, and its austere, implacable coast have caught the imaginations of the artist-folk. The result is that Carmel has a great deal of temperament that originally was not indigenous. At present it is a hotbed of soulful culture, a vortex of animated erudition. The artistic bacilli are so numerous that inoculation is imminent even to the visiting pachyderm.

Of late it has become the magnetizing center for writers, near writers, notsonear writers, distant writers, poets, poetines, artists, daubers, sloydists, and those aspiring ladies who spend their days smearing up with paint what would otherwise be very serviceable pieces of canvas. In addition, there are at least twenty college professors, a club of well-meaning neophytes of the arts-and-crafts, eso-

houses as they passed: "Come, the sunset!"

When the beach was reached, they seated themselves along a lupined hummock of posies; and what they did to that sunset was a-plenty. It was an adjectival orgy. One fair young thing, gazing rapturously, intoned the following:

"'Tis like a wassailous Bacchante, reeling her weltering rout."

"'Tis as a Cyclopean blacksmith," corrected Mary Austin, remembering her Browning, "striking frenzied sparks from the anvil of the horizon."

"Isn't it sweet?" (Was it Lucia Chamberlain's voice?)

Here London entered the commentative ring. "Sweet? Hell! That sunset has guts!"

The conversation then ascended into words of five syllables and over. So I retreated to Pine Inn and inquired for Alice MacGowan. Translating the directions into every-day English by the use of a pocket dictionary, with which I had armed myself before my invasion, I wandered off down the beach toward the large and imposing house situated on a hill overlooking the Carmel bay.

When Miss MacGowan appeared she

and also Mary Austin. The habits of this faction are impeccable. Bedtime at 10 o'clock, and nothing more inhibitional than milk in the way of liquid febrifuges. To this faction a cigarette is the symbol of the devil; and unconventionalities are the Old Boy's insidious artifices. The sunsets and the old homely virtues for them. No sporty vocal ensembles in tonsorial harmonics concerning "O you kid," and kindred subjects, could tempt them from the virtuous serenity of their ways.

The attitude of the outsiders—that is,

This 1910 *Los Angeles Times* article made fun of Carmel and its hedonistic artists colony. Courtesy of the *Los Angeles Times*.

at Point Lobos. Hers was the first of several such deaths in Sterling's immediate circle of friends.

In fact, the notion of suicide wasn't alien to Sterling. Early in their friendship, London, Sterling and Rogers talked about a suicide pact. In Adela Rogers St. Johns' book, *Final Verdict,* she described the discussion on page 363. Referring to Jack London, she wrote:

He got up in a tigerish leap. He put out one hand to my father, one to George Sterling. He said, 'Let us make a compact.'

'Let us agree not to sit up with the corpse,' he said.

'When our work is done, our lifeforce spent, exit laughing,' he said, persuading them, almost coaxing them. Is it a promise? We hereby agree not to sit up with the corpse.'

In time, Ambrose Bierce's influence on Sterling lessened. Sterling wrote "A Wine of Wizardry," and "Lilith," about a mythical witch, and gained even greater fame from this work. Sterling later met Robinson Jeffers and became one of his few personal friends.

By 1910, Carmel had gained a reputation for freedom and eccentricity. A *Los Angeles Times* article written by Willard Huntington Wright caught the moment. It was entitled "Hotbed of Soulful Culture, Vortex of Erotic Erudition: Carmel in California, where Author and Artist Folk are Establishing the Most Amazing Colony on Earth." From 1906–1916, it *was* that, but things began to change and dark shadows loomed over the colony.

In 1916, Jack London died of an overdose of morphine while having one of his kidney attacks. His friend "Greek" had a difficult time with his

death. Two years later, Sterling was dealt an even greater blow when his wife, Carrie, committed suicide. He struggled to accept her death, and finally returned to San Francisco and the Bohemian Club.

In 1926, Sterling took his own life with cyanide at the Club, just as he and London had agreed. Several lines of poetry were strewn around the room stating he had been to a dark side that no one understood.

By the time the well-known muckraker, Lincoln Steffens, came to Carmel in 1927, the real colony had disappeared. Steffens entertained guests such as Ernest Hemingway and Gertrude Stein, who visited his house on San Antonio Street.

Steffens also knew John and Carol Steinbeck, and suggested that Steinbeck write a series of articles for the *San Francisco News* about the Oklahoma immigrants and how they were treated in Monterey County. Over the next four years, those articles led to Steinbeck's writing *The Grapes of Wrath.*

Jack Kerouac, of San Francisco's beat generation, spent a brief time in Carmel. He had been directly involved in the anti-establishment movement that started in New York in the early 1950s. His 1962 book, *Big Sur,* about a cult leader moving to Big Sur, discussed other issues that were important to beats: jazz, drugs and sex.

Writers still gather in Carmel today. Usually you can find several of the town's notable authors at the Village Corner Restaurant each afternoon discussing their work and visiting with friends. Local award–winning mystery writers Robert Irvine and Robert Campbell meet there often.

Carmel had become home to many literary luminaries. Some stayed for years, while others like Robert Louis Stevenson visited for but a short time.

THE LUMINARIES: *Robert Louis Stevenson*

Robert Louis Stevenson left his Scottish homeland and followed Fanny Osbourne, a married woman, to California in 1879. Ten years his senior, Osbourne traveled with her two children, Isobel and Lloyd.

Rosanna Leese's Monterey boarding house became Stevenson's home while he waited for Osbourne to decide whether she would divorce her

Robert Louis Stevenson. Courtesy of the Mayo Hays Library.

husband, Sam Osbourne. While struggling to rid himself of his depression and emotions about Osbourne, Stevenson often wandered around the Monterey cemetery. At other times, he frequented a popular cafe in Monterey, owned by a white-haired Frenchman, Jules Simoneau. Simoneau, who welcomed and loved people, was considered something of a philospher and Stevenson wrote and published many letters about him.

Simoneau's was a gathering place for various ethnic groups. Whaling captains, sailors, and others of Spanish, French, English, or Portuguese descent would eat together there.

Stevenson was called Tusitalia, an Indian word meaning teller of tales. The Robert Louis Stevenson School in Pebble Beach had a student literary newspaper called *Tusitalia* and a snack bar called Simoneau's.

Stevenson was, of course, a prolific writer of essays and books, and many times wrote about the Carmel area. In an essay titled "The Old Pacific Capitol," he described the Carmel Mission ruins and referred to preservation of the Mission, saying the missionaries had accomplished good deeds there. He also expressed concern for the plight of the Indians, writing that no one cared about them since the Americans took over the area.

He described the San Carlos Day festival in "A Barbarian at the Carmel Mission." His book *Treasure Island* included a description of the Carmel shore and the Chinese fishermen at Pescadero fishing camps. In his essay "Silverado Squatters–The Sea Fog," Stevenson claimed that he left the Scottish seaboard to get away from the fog, but later welcomed the fog when he re-established himself in California.

Stevenson was well liked, but poor. His shoes were repaired by a Mexican man, a former pearl diver named Señor Bajores, who was proud to help the author. Jules Simoneau tried to help Stevenson earn money by suggesting he write for the *Monterey Californian.* Shortly thereafter, the writer became employed by that paper at $2.00 per week, which was actually paid by Simoneau and his friends.

The author was quiet but did have a good sense of humor. In 1879, editor Crevole Bronson, Simoneau, and an Italian fisherman from Monterey conspired against Father Antonio Cassanova, the priest who was raising money for the Carmel mission renovation.

Because the priest was known to be stingy, Stevenson wrote about an Italian man who knocked at the priest's door because they were both from the same Swiss–Italian village. The priest gave the man two bits—a quarter—and told him to ask his fishermen friends for more help. Stevenson called the priest "Father Two-Bits."

His relationship with Osbourne's son, Lloyd, was an affectionate one. Lloyd gave the author the nickname of "Luly." Stevenson wanted Lloyd to know the world and analyze people quickly. He told Lloyd that people in gold glasses hid behind them because they were dishonest and hypocrites. Lloyd said it was good they were so easy to spot!

After several months in Carmel, Stevenson left with Fanny Osbourne for San Francisco, where they finally married.

Robinson Jeffers

The brooding figure of poet Robinson Jeffers was an enigmatic presence in Carmel. Jeffers moved to Carmel in 1916 where he and his wife, Una Call Kuster, raised their two sons. Una had once been married to Edward Kuster, creator of Carmel's Golden Bough Theater, and in an act of spite, Kuster built a house that looked right into the Jeffers' bedroom window!

Jeffers built their home—called Tor House—near the ocean, an undertaking that took five years. The structure was built of native stone as well as stones collected from various trips Jeffers took over the years. Jeffers's son, Donnan, describes some of the stones Jeffers collected for the house in "The Stones of Tor House." Some stones came from Europe and each had a distinct history. One stone was found by Una and Robin, as the poet was affectionately called by friends and family, in Taos, New Mexico where they spent summers. The house had a staircase leading to Jeffers's study, Hawk Tower, with a view to the Pacific Ocean. In the turret of the tower are two portholes salvaged from ships. One of the portholes was from the *Inconstant,* later named *Natalia,* which Napoleon boarded in his narrow escape from Elba. It was shipwrecked in Monterey Bay in 1830. The other porthole was from a shipwreck that occurred off the coast of Pacific Grove in the late 1800s.

At one time, Jeffers was said to have poured wine from a barrel through the tower's gargoyles. The altar stone where Mary Austin played out her spiritual ceremonies is located only a few feet from Tor House near the beach.

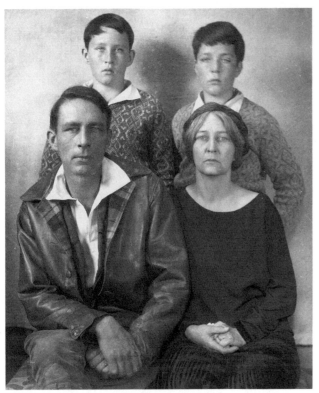

Robinson Jeffers poses with wife Una and twin sons Donnan and Lee. Courtesy of the Pat Hathaway Collection.

The Jeffers home—Tor House—was made of stone and featured this tower with a view of the Pacific. Courtesy of the Pat Hathaway Collection.

Few people were allowed in the Jeffers' home. One special friend and guest was Ansel Adams, the famed photographer, who played their Steinway grand piano and shared his views about nature.

Una handled Jeffers's business matters, provided him with social opportunities to meet people, and stayed close to him throughout their lives in Carmel. Supposedly, he supported the family from an inheritance, but actually his writing was his primary source of income.

Jeffers loved nature, especially the mountains and ocean. In "Notes About Places" which was part of his *Californians,* he described Carmel and wrote about the Indians and ranchers. He described the dark forests in "The Deer Lay Down Their Bones."

His 1924 liberal poem "Tamar" was hotly con-troversial because of its pagan and immoral views, which few dared to express at the time. In that poem, the heroine performs an obscene dance on the beach, imagining that she's been violated by Indian spirits who lived there before the white men destroyed them.

Jeffers's friends, Lincoln Steffens and George Sterling, both praised and criticized his work at the same time, along with many other commentators of the day. His collection *The Roan Stallion* received acclaim while in 1927 he was criticized for *The Women of Point Sur* in which he prophesied about the future and wrote of freedom. His 1933 work *Give Your Heart to the Hawks and other Poems* touched the same subject matter.

Because he wrote and talked about nature and preserving the environment, Jeffers was considered ahead of his time. He believed Carmel people actually lived among the natural beauty as people did in Homer's Greece.

Many thought Jeffers was a depressed man who didn't care for people. A 1935 article in the Tor House Newsletter, which was reprinted from the October 1935 issue of *Aperitif,* described a woman called Helen who claimed to be the Helen whom Jeffers wrote about in his poems. The article, which was written by John G. Moore, said that a woman named Helen romantically rejected Jeffers, and he then became a writer of dark poetry and a pessimist.

Jeffers did in fact know a woman named Lenore M. whom he referred to as Helen. However, Jeffers personally responded to the allegations in a letter and point-by-point disclaimed Helen's remarks. Jeffers said he often used the name "Helen" in his work of fiction and non-fiction. Apologies were forthcoming from the magazine's editor but Jeffers's dark mood persisted.

Jeffers was revered in the 1920s, but his gloomy writing proved too much for the 1930s Depression era, and interest in his work waned. In 1946, he wrote *Medea* and it was produced in New York starring Dame Judith Anderson, who had performed in his *The Tower Beyond Tragedy* in 1941.

He addressed the Library of Congress in 1942 and was asked to be the first Poet Laureate, but declined. The honor was bestowed instead upon Robert Frost.

Jeffers died in Carmel in 1962; members of the family still reside in the area.

Henry Miller

Not many people in Carmel mention Henry Miller, the controversial author and painter. Miller was a liberal socialist, and his writing was too sexually explicit for the more conservative Carmel residents.

In 1944 Miller fell in love with Big Sur after touring the area with artist Janko Varda. Varda showed Miller Anderson Creek where workers who built the Coast Highway project had once lived. The area was home to several artists for a time, but few seemed to stay very long. Miller

Author Henry Miller with his young wife Janina Lepska and daughter Valentine in the 1940s. Courtesy of the Henry Miller Library. Photo by Emil White.

wondered if it was because Big Sur had too much or too little sun, fog or peace.

Miller was introduced to Lynda Sargeant, who happened to have an extra room in her log house. Miller lived in her home for two months. The house was later the home of actors Orson Welles and Rita Hayworth and is today Nepenthe's, a popular Big Sur restaurant.

Although residents had their doubts, Miller claimed his relationship with Sargeant was purely platonic. After his *Tropic of Cancer* was published, however, his reputation as a sexual obsessive was cast, and it was difficult to believe he could be "just friends" with any woman. Miller was robust, outgoing, and considered oversexed by many people. In 1944, Miller married Janina Lepska, a young woman in her 20s.

Many women came and went in Miller's life after his marriage to Lepska ended. He did have two children, Valentine and Tony, with whom he spent a great amount of time in Big Sur.

The occult interested Miller, so he was pleased when he met Jean Wharton, who was reputed to be a white witch. She offered Miller the use of her home in Partington Ridge after she moved out, with the promise that he would not have to pay her anything until he became rich. He accepted. He lived there until 1957, having purchased the house outright with money she predicted would come to him.

He described his life there in his book *Big Sur and the Oranges of Hyeronymous Bosch.* Miller might have been called the "New Age" aficionado of his time. His interest in the occult and astrology grew,

and he was especially drawn to stories of flying saucers. According to Miller, flying saucers were sighted in Big Sur on many occasions. In fact, he witnessed what appeared to be two gyrating stars over the ocean one day.

Big Sur's natural mystical aura made the area a comfortable place for him. There was solitude, the sounds of the sea, the fog, and the mountains.

In 1944, three months after Miller moved to Big Sur, Emil White decided to move there, too. Miller had met White in 1920 when they both worked at the New York office of Western Union and years later they met again in Chicago.

In Big Sur, White lived in a nearby cabin and served as a bodyguard for Miller, keeping unwelcome visitors away. White and Miller were close friends throughout the years. Miller encouraged White to use his talents as an artist. White painted and wrote several travel guidebooks. White's cabin later became the Henry Miller Library, a cultural center that contains Miller's paintings and first editions of his books.

The Big Sur Land Trust took legal possession of the Henry Miller Library in 1981. Emil White lived in the cabin and operated the library until his death in 1989 when the Big Sur Land Trust took over its operation. Plans for the library's expansion and preservation of Miller's work continue to be developed.

Besides his earlier controversial works *Tropic of Cancer* and *Tropic of Capricorn,* the author is also known for such books as *Quiet Days in Clichy* and his *Henry Miller: Letters to Anais Nin,* which became the basis for a 1991 movie *Henry and June.* His letters are amassed 75 linear feet deep in a collection at the University of California at Los Angeles.

Miller died on June 7, 1980 in Pacific Palisades, California.

John Steinbeck

The name Steinbeck is immediately linked to such famous literary work as *The Grapes of Wrath, Of Mice and Men, The Red Pony,* and *Tortilla Flats.*

John Steinbeck was born in 1902 in Salinas, a town east of Monterey. Later he spent much of his time writing in the family's small Pacific Grove cottage built by his father in 1900, where he lived in 1930 with his wife, Carol. The author came and went from the area many times and lived in several houses. In 1941, he wrote the *Sea of Cortez* in Pacific Grove. After separating from Carol, he moved to New York with Gyndolyn Congler and became a war correspondent. When the author returned to California, he lived in the Soto House on Pierce Street in Monterey for a short time. He had married actress Gwen Verdon, whom he later divorced. Steinbeck returned to the family's Pacific Grove cottage and wrote *Zapata* in 1948. He researched *Cannery Row, Sweet Thursday* and *Tortilla Flats* at the cottage, and married Elaine Scott, former wife of actor Zachary Scott.

Many local people criticized Steinbeck because he drew his characters from the area residents. He became suspect every time he wrote because people wondered who would be in his next books. *East of Eden* was based on his family and Salinas. *Tortilla Flats* was about local Monterey residents and the tidal basins along the coast. *Pastures of Heaven,* writ-

Nobel Prize-winning author John Steinbeck was born in Salinas and moved to and from the area many times. Courtesy of the Pat Hathaway Collection.

ten in 1932, was based on an area east of Monterey called Corral de Tierra which, in 1776, was originally named Las Pasturas del Cielo by a Spanish soldier. He wrote about the Santa Lucia Mountains and redwood trees in his short story "Flight." *To a God Unknown* and *Cannery Row* were written about Monterey locals as well.

His friendship with Ed "Doc" Ricketts, a marine biologist, and founder of Monterey's Doc Ricketts Lab, was a long one. Steinbeck used Ricketts as a character in *Cannery Row,* and allowed Ricketts to be the first person to read the book. Years later, in the

1950s, the actual lab was purchased by the group of men who started the Monterey Jazz Festival.

Steinbeck was most influenced by Sir Thomas Malory's *Mort d'Arthur*. He became possessed by a need to continue a lifelong pursuit of the Holy Grail, a theme that occasionally underlies his writing. His unfinished work, *The Acts of King Arthur and his Noble Knights,* was posthumously published in 1976.

Because of Steinbeck's attempts at translating the Malory work, the John Steinbeck Arthurian Society was founded by Richard Andelson, with Steinbeck's friend Douglas Fairbanks, Jr. serving as Honorary Chairman. Steinbeck's Pacific Grove cottage on Central Avenue is now a museum, and the Steinbeck Society, based in Salinas, sponsors a Steinbeck Festival there. His work is performed at the Forest Theater each season. The Steinbeck Center Foundation in Salinas is breaking ground in 1994 for a new building that will house Steinbeck memorabilia.

Steinbeck was awarded the Nobel Prize in 1962 and the 1940 Pulitzer Prize for *The Grapes of Wrath*. The author died in New York in 1968, but his ashes were returned to Salinas.

Others

Several popular contemporary authors have lived in the area in recent years. Famed author Ernest K. Gann lived in Pebble Beach before moving to the northwest where he died in 1991. He wrote *Fate is the Hunter, The High and the Mighty,* and *Soldier of Fortune* among many others.

Alison Stilwell, the daughter of General Joseph "Vinegar Joe" Stilwell, who helped the Chinese flee from Japan, was the Pebble Beach author of *Chinese Cricket*.

The author of *Beaches,* Iris Rainer Dart, lived in Pebble Beach with her family. Novelist Roy Chanslor, a Pebble Beach resident, was the author of *The Ballad of Cat Ballou*.

Two popular and award-winning Carmel mystery writers, Robert Campbell and Robert Irvine, are active in the community. During Carmel's 1986 mayoral campaign, they served as co-chairmen of the incumbent Charlotte Townsend's campaign. Campbell was nominated for an Academy Award for his screenplay, *The Man of a Thousand Faces*. He's known as a crime novelist and has won the Edgar Allen Poe award from the Mystery Writers of America. Movie rights to his novel, *Alice in La-La Land,* were recently optioned.

PAINT BRUSHES

The Carmel coast was a popular place for the earliest of painters. In 1775, the Spanish artist Cristobal Diaz was the first to paint in the area, choosing the Carmel Mission as his subject. French artist Gasparo Duche de Vancy came to Carmel with Perouse's expedition in 1786.

In the 1800s, French artist Jules Tavernier stayed at Jules Simoneau's with several of his friends who painted in the area for a while. John Ross Key, the painter and son of Francis Scott Key of national anthem fame, arrived in 1873. Thomas Hill was another of the early artists whose works became popular in Carmel.

By the early 1900s painters Charles Rollo Peters, Xavier Martinez, Charles Dickman, Evelyn McCormick and Mary deNeale Morgan had come to the Carmel area. Ferdinand Burgdorff, Jo Mora and Thomas McGlynn lived in Pebble Beach. Famed marine painters William Ritschel and Paul Dougherty lived in the Carmel Highlands. Those two artists along with Arthur Hill Gilbert and Armin Hansen became members of the National Academy of Design.

Muralist Donald Teague moved to Carmel in 1949 and was once president of the Carmel Art Association. His work was exhibited in New York at the Metropolitan Museum of Art and the Watercolor Society of London. Teague lived in Carmel until his death in December 1991; a special exhibit of his work was held in Carmel in 1992.

A 1906 fundraiser called the Carmel Whirl benefitted local artists. The Hotel Del Monte opened an art gallery in 1907 which featured works by local artists. In 1927, nineteen artists met at Josephine Culbertson's studio and formed the Carmel Art Association. Pedro Lemos was the group's first president. The association sponsored lectures, concerts and art scholarships. One of its major fundraising events was the Bal Masque, a masked ball held at the Hotel Del Monte. The association also had traveling art shows.

Meetings included well-known guest artists such as George Bellows, Matteo Sandona and Sutton Palmer. Mrs. Nellie Comstock was the first patron to donate to the building fund. Her daughter, Carmel Valley artist Catherine Seideneck, spent summers in Carmel sculpting and making jewelry. Her brother, Hugh Comstock, designed and built Carmel's famed "Hansel and Gretel" cottages.

Popular Carmel artist Armin Hansen was known for his seascapes. The Monterey Peninsula Museum of Art contains an extensive collection of his work. Courtesy of the Pat Hathaway Collection.

Carmel became enamored with artists and a new era began. In the 1920s and 30s, Armin Hansen was considered *the* teacher of art, and founded the Carmel Art Institute. It was later brought under the direction of John Cunningham, who arranged for the first modern art exhibit on the peninsula. Hansen's characteristic seascape paintings are featured in the Jane and Dustin Dart wing of the Monterey Peninsula Museum of Art that was dedicated in 1993. A significant collection of his work was donated to the museum by the Darts of Pebble Beach.

James Fitzgerald, a watercolorist, arrived in 1919 and received an award for his "Reflections of a Sardine Fisherman" which was on exhibit at the Hotel Del Monte. He was highly praised for his seascapes and became active in Carmel's theater.

The Australian painter, Francis John McComas, was considered the "Whistler of the West." His career began as an illustrator in San Francisco before he and his second wife, Gene Baker, built their Pebble Beach home. He was a friend of Samuel Finley Brown Morse and well known in social circles. His work was part of the collection of the Metropolitan Museum of Art and his paintings of Monterey

Cypress trees are quite famous. McComas died in 1932, shortly after painting a mural for the Hotel Del Monte.

James Peter Cost, like many artists before him, said he belonged in Carmel, and in the 1950s painted at Mal Paso Creek, where he often hiked. The paintings of cypress trees and marine subjects by Carmel's Danny Garcia have been collected by Princess Margaret of Great Britain, and entertainers Steve Allen and Dean Martin.

Local artist Bill Dodge had already gained great

Artist Bill Dodge's popular folk painting of Carmel (1986) was later made into a jigsaw puzzle. The Dodge Gallery has been home to many local artists' work. Courtesy of Bill Dodge, the Bill Dodge Gallery.

popularity for his cityscapes of New York and San Francisco when he painted "Carmel," a folklife painting. In 1986, the painting was published as a limited-edition poster. In 1989 he issued a puzzle of the painting which sold out immediately and brought Dodge greater popularity. Dodge is also known for his willingness to help other artists.

Carmel now has approximately 70 art galleries. In the 1970s and 80s, the galleries relied heavily on Texas tourists who purchased the very expensive paintings on exhibit. Since 1990, however, these significant sales have declined and the town no longer seeks additional galleries.

CARTOONISTS

Fortunately, no matter what happens, there are some people who take life as lightly as possible, mainly cartoonists. Carmel certainly has its share of award winners.

Hank Ketcham, creator of "Dennis the Menace," moved to the Carmel Woods area in 1948 and then left in 1959. He had tired of Connecticut living about the same time Virgil Paul of the Walt Disney Studios called him to do some work for them. Ketcham said he is fortunate to be able to work in any part of the world and chose to move to Pebble Beach in 1977 after a long stay in Europe. Over the years, he's played in several Bing Crosby and AT&T golf tournaments in Pebble Beach.

His Pebble Beach studio was closed in the 1980s after residents complained that he was operating a commercial business in the community. He thereupon opened a studio next to Monterey's historic Colton Hall.

Hank Ketcham, creator of "Dennis the Menace." A Monterey Park is named after the character. Courtesy of the *Carmel Pine Cone.*

A movie based on Ketcham's cartoons premiered in Monterey on June 24, 1993. There is also a Dennis the Menace park at Lake El Estero in Monterey.

Bill Bates' work has appeared in the *Carmel Pine Cone* for more than 20 years. He has a way of reaching Carmel's pulse points. One cartoon depicted a Carmel police squad car as a cash register with a meter maid writing a ticket. After all, Carmel's reputation for giving the fastest parking tickets is widely known. Tourists often take home one or more of those paper souvenirs along with T-shirts and postcards.

Bates is originally from Tyler, Texas, but admits that his first love is Carmel and his second is the Fiji Islands. Eighteen of his cartoons are on permanent display at the Carmel Post Office and his work may

Drawing by Bill Bates.

"How come you never came to see me when I lived in Torrance?"

Cartoonist Bill Bates has Carmel's pulse. His cartoons have appeared in the *Carmel Pine Cone* for 20 years, and his work is on permanent exhibit at the Carmel post office.

be seen at the Dodge Gallery in Carmel also. He and artist Carol Minou completed a humorous mural of Carmel to celebrate Carmel's 75th birthday. The mural is located on the corner of San Carlos and Seventh Streets next to Nielsen's Market.

Bates is called the "cartoon laureate," according to Glenn Bernhardt of Carmel, chairman of the Northern Chapter of the National Cartoonists Society which was founded in 1990.

Eldon Dedini was born in Monterey County and attended Hartnell College in Salinas. He worked for Universal and Walt Disney Studios before freelancing for such notable publications as *Sports Illustrated* and *The Saturday Evening Post*. He received national recognition and continues to draw for *Esquire, The New Yorker* and *Playboy* magazines.

Another popular local cartoonist is Gus Ariola who created "Gordo." Dedini and Ariola are frequently seen at social events throughout the Peninsula.

Alex Anderson, the Pebble Beach resident and award-winning animator, is the creator of "Bullwinkle" and other animated series like "Crusader Rabbit." Preston Blair, an award–winning animator, lives in Carmel. Carmel's Vaughn Shoemaker won the Pulitzer Prize for his editorial cartoons in the *Monterey Peninsula Herald* and *San Francisco Examiner*.

Carmel's Tally Ho Inn was once the residence of another well–known cartoonist, Jimmy Hatlo. His creations, "Little Iodine" and "They'll Do It Every Time" were carried by hundreds of newspapers throughout the world. He and his wife Eleanor lived in the residence for six years before moving to their Pebble Beach house called "Wits End" along the golf course.

PHOTOGRAPHERS

Photographers have long enjoyed a bounty of subject matter in the Carmel area. Arnold Genthe came from San Francisco with the early artists in 1908 and was a colorful figure who enjoyed horses, women, and his freedom, though not necessarily in that order. He was active in Sterling's party scene and never married. His book, *As I Remember,* was filled with photographs of women.

Genthe later moved to New York, supposedly because he ran out of women to photograph.

Famed photographer Edward Weston lived in the Carmel Highlands from 1938–1958. He began his career in 1906 taking children's portraits in Los Angeles. Later he gained fame for his magnificent landscapes and still lifes of quite common subjects, including vegetables that, according to some observers, seemed to take on human qualities.

He and his first wife, Flora May Chandler, were married in 1909 and had four sons: Chandler, Brett, Neil, and Cole. In 1938 Weston married Charis Wilson. During the war years of 1941–1944, Weston was an airplane spotter in Carmel.

Weston died in 1958, but his sons, Cole and Brett, both gained fame as photographers. Brett concentrated on plant and beach subjects and was considered a great photographer. At the age of eighteen his work was on exhibit at San Francisco's M. H. de Young Museum.

Shortly before he died in Kona, Hawaii on January 22, 1993, Brett Weston destroyed all of his negatives as his father had done with his work from 1906-1921. Brett said that no one could print them like he could. His ashes were returned to Carmel.

Cole Weston, who admits that his first love is the theater, is not only a highly regarded photographer but also a popular Carmel resident. He lives near Big Sur and enjoys sailing his boat. He gained recognition in Carmel as the Executive Director of the Carmel Sunset and Cultural Center and for his work with the Forest Theater Guild. Cole served as president and has been a Guild board member

Cole Weston. Photograph by Monica Von Stackelberg, courtesy of Cole Weston.

for forty-five years. He often directs plays there including many of Steinbeck's work.

Cole credits his brother Brett and his father for helping him gain actual working experience. He never had a formal lesson. He made his first photo in 1927. In 1988 he stopped printing his father's negatives and directed his attention to his own work and career.

Ansel Adams first visited Carmel in 1926 with Albert Bender, a philanthropist and benefactor of the arts. Adams met Robinson and Una Jeffers on that first trip and stayed in the Carmel Highlands where he eventually built a home. His friends included Jehanne Salinger Carlson of Pacific Grove, the mother of President John F. Kennedy's Press Secretary, Pierre Salinger. He was also friends with Edward Weston and Mary Austin, who wrote the text of Adams's 1930s book, *Taos Pueblo*. Adams developed the "zone system" of photography and became famous for his magnificent landscapes in Yosemite and New Mexico. In Carmel Cole Weston provided space in the Sunset Center for Adams's photography association, Friends of Photography.

Another accomplished photographer from the area is Morely Baer of Big Sur, who has written and published photographic books about the Big Sur

Virginia Adams, wife of Ansel Adams, at their Carmel Highlands home. Courtesy of the photographer Kathleen Olson.

and Monterey areas, among them *The Wilder Shore*.

FOOTLIGHTS IN THE FOREST

Theater has played an important part in Carmel's community, many times with conflict and hilarity. Practically every Carmel resident has been involved in the local theater productions, either on stage, as part of the audience, or both—sometimes at the same performance.

The Forest Theater is the oldest of California's legitimate outdoor theaters. In the early days, artists, residents, and commercial business owners all worked together on these productions. Everyone got into the act!

As a Carmel newcomer, Herbert Heron Peet, preferably known as Bert Heron, shared his thoughts and enthusiasm about starting a theater with James Franklin Devendorf. The developer offered to lease an entire block of forested land for the project, and the Forest Theater began in 1910.

The theater still stands on the original site at Forest Avenue and Mountain View. Beyond the wooden gates, guests enter a magical theater which comes alive at the evening performances when the stage is transformed into a castle or old western town. The stage is set in a natural amphitheater backdrop with the woods and ocean beyond. Originally, there were two large pine trees that grew on either side of the stage, forming a natural picture frame. The beauty of the setting lends itself to the performances when the fog rolls through or the full moon lights the theater. Although the log seats have been replaced, guests still warm themselves by fires set at either end of the stage.

Herbert Heron Peet, pictured here in the 1916 production of "The Black Arrow," founded Carmel's Forest Theater. Courtesy of the Local History Department, Harrison Memorial Library.

The idea behind the theater was that it would be a place for local and California talent to have their work performed. *David* was the first production and included such locals as Glenn Leidig's parents and Bert Heron. Ferdinand Burgdorff designed the set.

Having so many artists working together often created conflicts and feuds about how plays would be produced. Sterling and Heron charged Perry

Newberry with plagiarism of the play *The Toad.* It was produced anyway in 1912. Newberry won over Heron when his play *Junipero Serra* was produced and well-liked by the community.

George Sterling and Heron banded together against Newberry on several occasions and eventually formed another theater group called The Western Drama Society. Mary Austin produced her play, *Fire,* with this group. Watercolor artist James Fitzgerald played the title role in *Julius Caesar.*

Forest Theater players were known to drink too much on occasion, which often resulted in someone being knocked over accidentally or part of the set falling down. Harry Leon Wilson suggested that someone write a book about all the amusing incidents that happened in Carmel. He wouldn't do it, he said, because he wanted to stay in Carmel and because he couldn't afford additional house insurance! He claimed the Forest Theater was a group of amateurs.

During one production, Harry Wilson watched his wife in a love scene with Theodore Criley and became furious. Ten months later, seething with jealousy, he challenged Criley to a fight and lost. His wife left him anyway five years later.

The Arts and Crafts Theater, a spin-off of sorts with an indoor facility for plays during the colder months, was the third theater group formed.

In 1924, Edward Kuster originated The Golden Bough Theater where guests sat in wicker chairs under an extensive domed ceiling. A theater school was conducted there. At one time it was considered one of the country's loveliest small theaters. Carmel provided theatrical opportunities for performers

Top: For more than 70 years, the Forest Theater has provided entertainment for Carmel residents and visitors. Bottom: early guests at Kuster's Golden Bough sat in wicker chairs. It's now a movie theater. Courtesy of the Local History Department, Harrison Memorial Library.

and playwrights during these early years.

The Golden Bough burned in the 1930s as a result of an arson fire. Shortly thereafter, when his Studio Theater was destroyed by fire, there was rumor that someone didn't want Kuster in Carmel's theater business.

In 1920, the Forest Theater purchased the land it had leased from John Franklin Devendorf. Later the town of Carmel purchased the entire theater.

After a few years the Forest Theater, Arts and Crafts Theater and Western Drama Society joined together as one again.

During the depression years, the theaters were quiet, and during World War II the only light on stage came from the moon.

Robinson Jeffers's play, *The Tower Beyond Tragedy,* interested the actress Judith Anderson and was performed by her at the Forest Theater in 1941. It was such a great success that a short time later, in 1942, Jeffers's play opened in New York to wonderful reviews. Jeffers became a recognized playwright and again Carmel was in the national limelight.

In 1950, Bert Heron organized the Forest Theater Guild in order to raise money for its productions. Performances were less frequent in the ensuing years. By 1971, Mayor Barney Laiolo and the City Council considered using the facility as a parking lot for city vehicles. Cole Weston, one of the Theater Guild's founders, couldn't stand to see the theater turned into a parking lot. Money needed to be raised and he persuaded Judith Anderson to perform a reading from the Jeffers play. Because it was a success, a performance of *Twelfth Night* followed, both proving the theater's significance.

A short time later, the city rescinded its parking lot idea and allocated money to the theater's first renovation. A contract exists today which allows the Forest Theater Guild first choice of theater dates ahead of any other performing groups that are allowed use of the facilities.

In 1987, renovation plans were revealed at a large fundraising party at the La Playa Hotel. Entertainment consisted of scenes from that summer's current productions. Although board members were wary of such a large event, it succeeded and provided the groundwork for future fundraising events, including fashion shows by known designers. These events continue to involve the public in support of the theater.

IV
Architecture

The Carmel area has an outstanding and unique array of architectural styles. The Indians' grass and mud huts set the example for California's early architecture, especially the adobe buildings. When wood was difficult to obtain because of labor shortages, native stone became widely used as time went on.

The original log buildings at the Mission San Carlos de Borromeo became the base of the Mission's sandstone construction in 1793. The Moorish architectural design is easily recognized by the Mission's dome, star-like windows, and pyramid finials on the towers.

ADOBES

Monterey's first adobe two-story colonial was built by architect Thomas Larkin in 1835 at a reported cost of $5,000, and took three years to complete. Larkin was born in Boston, Massachusetts and became the United States Consul to California in 1845. He introduced the concept of a double veranda, which may have come from his years as a resident of the south. He was also reported to be the first designer to use wallpaper in a house. Ships' carpenters worked on the wood structure of the house, which has one hallway with rooms on either side. The house's style combines eastern seaboard and southern influences. In 1922, Larkin's granddaughter, Alice Larkin Thomas, bought the house and lived there until 1957. She gave the house to the State of California with an agreement that the house contain its original furnishings.

The Whaling Station in Monterey, built by Scott David Wight, originally served as headquarters for a group of Portuguese whalers. The Monterey County Junior League has decorated the building with period furnishings.

In 1830, one-story adobes were described by Richard Henry Dana in his book *Two Years Before The Mast*. The Casa de Soto is one of those. Another prominent Monterey adobe was California's first theater. Originally built as a saloon by Jack Swan in 1844, it still stands on the southwest corner of Scott and Pacific Streets.

The Custom House was the first public building in Monterey and has been completely restored. California's Magna Carta was signed in that building, which has become the centerpiece of the Custom House Plaza.

Cannery Row, where sardine canning was the biggest industry in Monterey, has been preserved and some of the old buildings have been incorporated into new designs. For example, the Hovden

The adobe Custom House in Monterey is the oldest government building west of the Rocky Mountains. Courtesy of the Mayo Hays Library.

Cannery, built in 1916, was the town's largest cannery, and was in use until 1972. Portions of the original structure have been incorporated into the Monterey Bay Aquarium.

The Aquarium was first proposed in 1977 by marine biologists from Stanford University's Hopkins Marine Station in Pacific Grove, and opened to the public on October 20, 1984. Philanthropist David Packard, co-founder of the Hewlett-Packard Corporation, and his wife, Lucile, donated $55 million to initiate construction of the facility.

The American Institute of Architects awarded the building's architects, Esherick Homsey Dodge and Davis, an honor for their design. Nearly 15 million people have visited the aquarium since it opened. The aquarium's three-story kelp forest gives visitors a diver's view of the sea. A 326,000-gallon tank is home to sharks and other fish.

HANSEL AND GRETEL

Carmel's architectural adobe treasures include the fairy-tale Hansel and Gretel cottages built in the 1920s by Hugh M. Comstock.

Comstock's wife, Mayotta Brown Comstock, was a doll maker popular for her "Otsy-totsy" dolls in the 1920s. As her collection of dolls outgrew their home, her husband designed and built the first "doll house," an adobe brick cottage painted in gray and green tones. A second cottage followed and the two cottages, Hansel and Gretel as they were called, took nearly six years to complete and cost about $400. Hansel was built on Torres be-

Architect and builder Hugh Comstock designed his fairy-tale-like cottages when his wife's doll collection became too large for their home. This Comstock adobe clearly shows the roofline, arches, and windows that exemplify the architect's style. Courtesy of the Pat Hathaway Collection.

tween Fifth and Sixth Streets, and Gretel on Torres and Santa Fe. Comstock also built the popular Tuck Box Tea Room on Dolores, between 7th and Ocean Avenue. The Comstock residence was built on Sixth Avenue between Santa Fe and Torres. Its double-door entry, stained glass window, and stone shingles were characteristic of his designs.

Carmel's "master builder," M. J. Murphy, earned that sobriquet for the quality of his workmanship. He was only seventeen years of age when he built his first house in 1902. The house was built around the tent where he, his mother and five sisters had been living. In the following years, he built the town's library, the Sundial Lodge, the Pine Inn and many other commercial buildings throughout the town. Murphy worked with James Franklin Devendorf and eventually started his own business, which included a lumber yard.

In 1992, amidst controversy, the first Murphy

Comstock adobes in Carmel include the Tuck Box Tea Room on Ocean Avenue. Such stylized cottages have given the town the reputation for being a fairy tale village. Courtesy of the Local History Department, Harrison Memorial Library.

Carmel's Harrison Memorial Library still looks much the same as it did in this 1930 photo. The building was designed by Bernard Maybeck and built by M.J. Murphy. Courtesy of the Local History Department, Harrison Memorial Library.

house was dedicated to the town of Carmel-by-the-Sea to be used as a community center. This act of preservation didn't cost the taxpayers anything because the funds were donated by the owner, Stella Biason.

Carmel's Harrison Memorial Library's stone structure and huge fireplace in the main reading room is a popular place for tourists and residents. The library was designed by architect Bernard Maybeck, who also designed homes in Pebble Beach. He served as architect, along with Julia Morgan, for Mrs. William R. Hearst in designing the Hearst Memorial Gymnasium for Women on the University of California Berkeley campus.

In Carmel Valley, the Casa Boronda was built of adobe on Rancho Los Laureles, land which had been granted to Jose Manuel Boronda and Vicente Blas Martinez in 1840.

From 1820 through 1920, the term "bungalow" was used to describe a house of great informality, usually a single-floor cottage. This was the style that made two brothers, Charles and Henry

Greene, famous. Their bungalows contained large living rooms, and halls of board and batten construction, similar to Japanese homes.

CHARLES SUMNER GREENE

Architect Charles Sumner Greene and his brother, Henry, gained popularity in Southern California after building the Gamble House, an expansive residence located in Pasadena, California. These innovators used wood to make homes simple in design but comfortable. Descending roof lines went beyond the walls, and open living areas with terraces were also part of their style.

Charles Greene was born in Cincinnati, Ohio in 1868 and Henry in 1870. They grew up in rural Virginia and this simple lifestyle influenced their designs. Both attended the Massachusetts Institute of Technology (MIT) in 1881 and two years later traveled to Pasadena. In 1952 the Greene brothers received a citation from the American Institute of Architects for their outstanding designs.

In 1915, Charles Sumner Greene left the firm

This photograph of the Charles Sumner Greene Studio in Carmel shows the arches inspired by the Mission San Antonio in Jolon, south of Carmel. The studio was built in 1923. Courtesy of Gordon Greene.

he and his brother established to move to Carmel. D. L. James commissioned Greene to build a house of Carmel stone in the Carmel Highlands. Construction began in 1917, and was completed four years later in an adobe mission architectural style to fit into a cliff site. The tile roof is easily visible as the building overlooks the Pacific Ocean.

Greene started work on his own studio, inspired by the villas of Italy, of frame construction and with leftover materials from the James House but he never completed it. Greene's son, Gordon Greene, obtained his architectural license and used his own

ideas and those of his father to complete the studio, a few blocks from downtown Carmel on Lincoln Street. He lives in the studio house with his wife, Bette. After the James project, Greene restored the residence of writer Martin Flavin in the Highlands, and the Langley Howard house in Monterey.

There were several interesting facets to Greene's designs. Gordon said his father felt that anything he built had to conform to the area and fit into the environment. The architect also designed furniture and gardens and hand-carved details in wood. In the Greene studio, some carvings stop at doorways, and none are the same.

Gordon Greene said his father made one side of a fireplace smaller and thinner than the other, thereby showing the male and female in everything. He said his father would take the conventional and put personality into the designs.

Greene recalled a nostalgic moment that occurred in Cornwall, England when he stood at the same archway that influenced his father's work. Gordon stood at the same spot, took a photograph, and said he felt very close to his father at that moment. A drawing of that original stone archway, made by his father in 1909, is displayed in the studio. The James House design includes several such archways as does the Greene studio, which were inspired by the ruins of *Tintagel*.

OTHER CARMEL STRUCTURES

Another unique Carmel home was one designed by Frank Lloyd Wright for Della Walker in 1954. The house resembles a ship turned upside down with a copper roof. It is located at the south end of Carmel Beach and is easily recognized. Wright designed the furniture, which is built into the walls. The kitchen resembles a ship's galley but has good natural light, glass, wood, and Carmel stone to interact with both the outdoors and indoors.

James Franklin Devendorf built the Door House on Lincoln Street right after San Francisco's 1906 earthquake. The house was built of molded wooden doors which were part of a shipment of building materials Devendorf received from San Francisco. He had no idea what the rest of the shipment contained, but used the doors for construction anyway. The house was originally owned by Pebble Beach's

Frank Lloyd Wright designed this residence on Carmel's Scenic Drive for Della Walker. Courtesy of the Pat Hathaway Collection.

first woman postmaster, Janet Carroll.

Carmel's Sunset and Cultural Center has been home to special symphony performances and the Bach Festival. The stone-and-brick building was designed by C. J. Ryland in 1906. In the late 1980s, a committee was formed to investigate the possibility of renovating and enlarging the center, but nearby residents were upset that the proposed changes would require additional parking. Parking meant more cars, of course, and more cars meant more people and so on.

Although the money for renovation was being donated by well-known area philanthropist Virginia Stanton, after months of discussion the idea was dropped. In 1993, the renovation issue arose again. This time the city would have to pay for any renovation. Environmental impact reports were completed, but to date no final decision has been made.

Another interesting building in the Carmel area is the Carmelite Monastery. In 1931, the Francis J.

Carmel's Sunset and Cultural Center was originally a school. Today it houses a 700-seat theater. Courtesy of the *Carmel Pine Cone.*

The Carmelite Monastery, commissioned and donated by the Sullivan family in the 1920s, is located on Highway One south of Carmel. Courtesy of the Pat Hathaway Collection.

Sullivan family hired architects Maginnis & Walsh to design and build the Romanesque and Spanish Colonial structure for the Carmelite nuns. The red tile roof, white stucco walls, and yellow stained-glass windows are easy to see on the hill overlooking the ocean on Highway One. The monastery is located across the highway from the dreaded Monastery Beach where many lives have been lost in the surf.

Another noteworthy residence is the large stone Mediterranean home on San Antonio Street that was once owned by Phil and Marie Gordon. She was an active member of the Forest Theater and he had been with the Southern Pacific Railroad. Materials were brought from Spain to build the house.

In 1992, prompted by members of the Carmel Heritage Society, a local history organization, an Architectural and Historical Survey was begun. The survey will document historic buildings throughout Carmel-by-the-Sea. The National Trust for Historic Preservation declared Carmel a "national treasure" in 1993.

Carmel residents take their trees seriously and many trees have been designated as historic, are numbered, and are protected from being cut down. In 1992, Friends of the Carmel Forest was formed to make residents aware of tree preservation.

PEBBLE BEACH ESTATES

Several Pebble Beach estates deserve mention, including the Griffin estate, a two-story wood home built in 1853 by John Gore. It was designed by George Washington Smith who also designed the Cypress Point Clubhouse. Many famous architects designed homes in Pebble Beach including Bernard Maybeck, Addison Mizner, and Clarence Tantau.

The Byzantine Castle at Pescadero Point on the 17 Mile Drive was built by Mrs. Helen Irwin Crocker. Courtesy of the Pebble Beach Company.

The Griffin estate was named "Cheviot Hill" for the Cheviot sheep that grazed there. When Mrs. Hately, one of the original owners, divorced her husband, actor Jonathon Hale, she married Allen Griffin, publisher of the *Monterey Peninsula Herald*. The home has lovely gardens and grounds and the house was the center of social activity until Mrs. Griffin's death in 1989.

The Templeton Crocker estate, more popularly known as the Byzantine Castle, was also designed by Smith, complete with arches, towers, and nat-ural stone. It is located well above the cliffs directly overlooking the ocean and was used for the 1979 Walt Disney production *Escape to Witch Mountain*.

Clarence Tantau designed the Leonard Firestone estate on the Pebble Beach golf course with its long, low styling. Lewis Hobart designed the 1918 main building of the Del Monte Lodge at Pebble Beach. Two other special homes are the Villa Cypress and Villa Felice on 17 Mile Drive where tourists stop to look at the outstanding Mediter-ranean designs. The elaborate stone buildings re-semble European castles and villas perched above the shoreline on craggy rock outcroppings.

THE HOTELS: *The Pine Inn*

This popular and historic inn was first the Hotel Carmelo built in 1887 by James Franklin Devendorf and Frank Powers with wood from the Tivoli Opera House in San Francisco. After 16 years, the Hotel Carmelo was rolled to the Pine Inn's present loca-tion on Ocean and Lincoln Streets.

The 49-room hotel tries to recreate Victorian charm even in "The Red Parlor" bar, a local hang-out. The red-and-white decor is carried throughout the popular tourist hotel. Earlier amenities, includ-ing tennis courts, have long since disappeared.

The lobby, where high tea is still served, con-tains antique period furniture. The hotel has had several owners over the years and some celebrities, including Bing Crosby, have been hotel guests.

The hotel is rumored to have a ghost, like many of the other Carmel area hotels, but no one seems bothered by it.

The Pine Inn's location was also the site of several early Carmel churches. A major renovation in 1992 did not change the hotel's charming ambiance. The restaurant is now operated by the Marriott Corporation.

The La Playa Hotel

Romance surrounds Carmel's most famous hotel, a revered place where many couples spend their honeymoons. The hotel's beginnings were equally romantic.

Christian Jorgensen, a Norwegian artist born in 1859, married Angela Ghiradelli of the famed San Francisco Ghiradelli family. She was Jorgensen's student at the School of Design in San Francisco (now called the California Artists Association). Jorgensen was known for his outstanding paintings of Yosemite and extensive studies of the Carmel Mission and he became famous for his *The Red Stack*

Newton Cope, Sr. owns the historic La Playa Hotel, which he renovated extensively in 1983. Courtesy of the *Carmel Pine Cone.*

The La Playa Hotel on Camino Real was originally a private residence built by artist Christian Jorgensen for his wife, Angela Ghiradelli, daughter of the San Francisco chocolate manufacturers. Courtesy of the Pat Hathaway Collection.

Row Boats. His work was given to the Bohemian Club of San Francisco after his death.

The hotel was originally designed by Jorgensen in 1902 as a mansion for his wife. The architectural style was of Spanish origin with stucco walls and beams brought in from Northern California. It was steam heated. (Hotel manager Tom Glidden says the heating system is haunted because of the interesting sounds made by the pipes.) The mansion originally had a stairway leading to a non-existent bell tower, a stairway that now leads to the second floor. Some of the original stonework is still obvious on the front exterior of the hotel.

In 1904, the Jorgensens moved into their house.

It was the first residence in Carmel to have a swimming pool, which was originally located where the Terrace Grill is today. The mansion had an outstanding view of Carmel Bay, Pebble Beach, and Point Lobos.

Although the Jorgensens were known for their warmth and hospitality, there are varying accounts of Mrs. Jorgensen's death. One has it that she drowned off Carmel Beach one year after their marriage, and that her husband couldn't bring himself to live there any more. Whatever the cause of her mysterious disappearance, Jorgensen leased the house to Agnes Alice Signor, who proceeded to add twenty rooms and rent them out. The hotel was then known as "The Strand."

In the 1920s, Harrison and Fred Godwin, Alice Signor's grand nephews, learned the business from her. After a fire destroyed part of the building, they added 30 more rooms during its renovation. Years later, Fred Godwin bought out his brother's interest in the hotel. He was mayor of Carmel from 1946 to 1950. He was killed in an auto accident in 1975.

A 1940 note to hotel guests stated the hotel management's approval of guests wearing sportswear to lunch, but coats and ties were definitely required at dinner.

In 1952 Godwin leased the hotel to Ashton Stanley, whose father was a famous California hotel owner.

In 1968, Bud Allen, a popular Carmel resident who owns several businesses, purchased the hotel from Godwin. Allen can be recognized wearing one of his plaid hats around town. Until 1993 he also owned "It's Bud's Pub," where locals and guests enjoyed Allen's off-beat sense of humor. Restaurant guests observed a white toy polar bear hanging upside down on the ceiling. The Pub was a popular retreat after the 1986–1988 city council meetings. It is now the site of the Red Lion restaurant.

Allen is known for his pranks, and several stories are credited to his name. He once offered $1000 to men who would shave off their mustaches, and did get a couple of takers. Another story has it that a baby alligator lived in the hotel's employee dining room during his ownership. One Christmas Eve, Allen put several white mice under his hat, tipped it to the ladies, and your imagination will tell you the rest. The Society for the Prevention of Cruelty to Animals (SPCA) didn't find this amusing, however.

Allen sold the La Playa to the prominent San Francisco Newton Cope family in 1983. Mr. Cope and his sons, Newton, Jr. and John, also own and operate the highly respected Huntington Hotel on Nob Hill in San Francisco. The La Playa Hotel is one of a number of hotels that are part of the National Trust for Historic Preservation.

After the Copes' purchase of the property, the hotel was extensively renovated. The owners wanted to paint the building a traditional Mediterranean pink, but the city objected at first. Shortly thereafter, approvals were given. An eight-month renovation was necessary for the run-down building and in July 1984, after spending $5 million, the Cope family opened the hotel.

The paneled wood walls in the hotel's Terrace Grill, the lobby, and restaurant are filled with historic photographs and posters which Mr. Cope has collected over the years. In fact, an outstanding collection of photographs from the Forest Theater is on display there.

In recent years, the hotel has been used for many interesting activities. It provided the location shots for the 1986 TV series "Simon and Simon." The scenes were supposed to represent locations in Latin America.

The garden and pool areas are lovely settings for many parties and weddings. The hotel's ballroom was the site for Carmel Mayor Clint Eastwood's 1986 victory celebration. The next day, the gazebo garden area was used for the new mayor's first major press conference.

The Highlands Inn

James Franklin Devendorf purchased 600 acres of land in the Carmel Highlands that had once been Rancho San Jose y Sur Chiquito, part of an old Mexican land grant. The area was first called the Highlands when Scottish sailors jumped ship. In 1916, Devendorf began building the hotel with local granite, and within a year the first guests enjoyed the facility. A few years later, he sold the Inn to Senator and Mrs. Edward H. Tickle and Ella Shaw Fisher, Mrs. Tickle's sister.

Ansel Adams, Jack London, and Pulitzer Prize-winning writer Martin Flavin were some of the early guests. After Highway One was completed in 1937, the inn was sold to Dudley Yard and Alexander Allen. Three years later, Robert J. Ramsey, a San Francisco hotel owner of Scottish heritage, purchased and remodeled the hotel. He and his wife, Patricia Smith Ramsey, owned the

The Highlands Inn built by Frank Devendorf has been popular since it opened in 1916. Courtesy of the Pat Hathaway Collection.

hotel. Three years after her husband's death in 1978, Mrs. Ramsey sold the hotel to architect Will Shaw, who was active in the Big Sur Land Trust.

The Hotel Del Monte

The elaborate Hotel Del Monte, with its Mediterranean design, opened in June 1880 after being under construction for 100 days at a cost of $1 million. The hotel contained 500 rooms and a spectacular dining hall, and became the world's largest resort. The building's character was preserved even after it was destroyed by fire on two occasions in 1887 and 1924.

The "Big Four," Charles Crocker, Collis P. Huntington, Mark Hopkins and Leland Stanford, who owned the Southern Pacific Railroad, built the hotel in Monterey on 126 acres of the 7000 acres they purchased from David Jacks. Ballrooms and telephones attracted wealthy travelers who journeyed on the Southern Pacific train to Monterey.

It remained a hotel until Samuel Finley Brown Morse, who later purchased the property from the

The Hotel Del Monte's elegant dining room served wealthy guests, many of whom traveled from the east coast. Courtesy of the Pat Hathaway Collection.

Big Four, gave it to the Navy in 1945 during World War II, when it became the home of the Naval Post Graduate School. In 1986, the Robert Louis Stevenson School's senior prom was held in the grand ballroom, which is occasionally used for special events.

The Mission Ranch

In 1986, after being elected mayor, Clint Eastwood rescued a piece of Carmel's history. He purchased the 22-acre Mission Ranch property, adjacent to the Carmel Mission, for approximately $5 million. In doing so, he saved the old seaside re-

sort from becoming the condominium development planned by the previous owners.

Eastwood is of Scottish descent, like the ranch's first owner, William Martin. The actor first visited the ranch in the 1950s when he was a soldier at Fort Ord during the Korean War.

During his term of office from 1986 to 1988, Eastwood occasionally stopped at the ranch, which was still a country resort, late in the evening and visited with local residents who enjoyed the ranch's informality. Because the ranch is outside the town's limits, live music is allowed and Eastwood, an ex-

Once a dairy farm in the late 1880s, Mission Ranch was purchased by Clint Eastwood in 1986 for about $5 million. Courtesy of the *Carmel Pine Cone.*

cellent jazz musician, plays the piano occasionally there. Former Carmel mayor Barney Laiolo has often played his gut-bucket during late Sunday night jam sessions there, too.

Eastwood's friend and restauranteur, John Purcell, moved to Carmel from Vail, Colorado to help Eastwood reorganize the facility. In 1992 Eastwood completed renovation of the ranch after being granted an amendment to the Monterey County Land Use Plan, a feat no average citizen could have easily accomplished. The plan restricted any changes

to the historic property, but Eastwood and Alan Williams, a local developer who works for the actor, attended numerous Planning Commission meetings where the actor told the commissioners he really cared about the property. He said he wanted to renovate the Mission Ranch, add parking, renovate the existing buildings, and maintain the property's character and integrity. Eastwood contracted with Angelo de Maria, the 77-year-old mason who, years before, had worked on the Templeton Crocker mansion in Pebble Beach.

The Monterey County Supervisors were ultimately responsible for making any final decision to approve the amendment. Monterey County Supervisor Sam Karas, who had been active in the area's theater scene for years, appeared in a bit part in Eastwood's Academy-Award-winning film *Unforgiven*. It was being shot on location while Eastwood's permit was pending. Rather than compromise his position on the Board of Supervisors, Karas disqualified himself from discussing the Mission Ranch issue to avoid facing conflict-of-interest charges. In fact, he donated his paycheck from the movie to the NAACP. Even so, some residents believe the role was a thank you for influencing the amendment change. That's Carmel!

Eastwood remodeled the existing ranch restaurant and leased it out. Shortly thereafter, letters of complaint appeared in the *Carmel Pine Cone* because the menu excluded more common items like ground sirloin steak which had been normal fare for years at the ranch. Notwithstanding such grievances, however, the ranch has become a popular informal, resort under Eastwood's direction.

V
Legends, Folklore, Ghost Stories and Scandal

The Carmel area's mystique includes extraterrestrial sightings, haunted buildings with their own personal ghosts, bandits, and a 1920s scandal that brought Carmel national attention.

SCANDAL

No other event created more national publicity in the early days than the alleged appearance in Carmel of Southern California evangelist Aimee Semple McPherson. She was one of the wailing-type preachers with a large temple and following in Los Angeles. Anthony Quinn and Marilyn Monroe were two of her many celebrity followers.

After a swim in the Pacific Ocean one day in May 1926 in Southern California, McPherson was reported missing. Witnesses said they saw her talking to a man on the beach that day. It was feared that she had drowned. They didn't hear whether she called him Denny or Benny but they did recall his definite odd way of walking. Divers searched but did not find her body.

The authorities received reports from people in various parts of California who said they had seen the preacher. Underworld figures said they were holding her for ransom but that was proven false.

McPherson had become friendly with her radio station's chief engineer, Kenneth Ormiston, a married man with two children. He disappeared at the same time as McPherson.

The *Sacramento Union* reported that a car registered to Ormiston was found in Carmel Valley. A reporter said he stopped a car south of Carmel near San Luis Obispo to ask directions of a man and woman heading north who fit the descriptions of McPherson and Ormiston.

One month later, McPherson was found in Arizona. She told everyone she had been kidnapped from the beach. In July, two months after her disappearance, Carmel made the national news when a report revealed that McPherson and Ormiston had really been staying in a Carmel cottage.

A man calling himself George McIntire had been shown a cottage on Scenic Drive by realtor Daisy Bostick of Carmel Realty. The man paid several months' rent in advance for himself and his supposed wife. Next-door neighbors, Jeannette and Percy Parkes, identified the pair as the missing evangelist and radio engineer. The owner of the

The Benedict Cottage in Carmel on Scenic Drive was the site of evangelist Aimee Semple McPherson's 1926 scandal. The stories that surfaced about her affair threw Carmel into the national limelight. Courtesy of the Pat Hathaway Collection.

house, Henry C. Benedict, identified McPherson's green bathing suit from a news description. He said she was dressed up in Carmel, which was totally out of place for most people in the area. He said that was how he recognized her.

A complaint was filed against McPherson, charging her with creating a hoax, perjury for saying she was kidnapped, and fraud. The case was tried in Southern California. At one point the trial was almost brought to Carmel, but the town's marshall, August C. England, wouldn't allow it.

At the trial, a bible purchased in a Carmel bookstore by a man identifed as Ormiston and a grocery receipt were key items in the case. When a juror,

E. A. Holmes, left the courtroom, the receipt mysteriously disappeared and couldn't be used as evidence.

Ralph Swanson and William McMichael identified them, too, but during the subsequent trial, McMichael denied seeing her. Ernest Rickert said he delivered wood to the cottage and identified the two people. A retired engineer, Ralph W. Hersey, testified to seeing McPherson on Ocean Avenue.

Benedict left Carmel after tiring of all the curiosity-seekers around his cottage on Scenic Drive. Did McPherson have an illicit affair with Ormiston in that Carmel cottage? Only the town residents really know and they wouldn't likely make it national news. Or would they?

GHOSTS AND THINGS

Ghosts seem to enjoy the Carmel area as much as everyone else. A lady in black has allegedly been sighted at the Robert Louis Stevenson House in Monterey. Supposedly, a docent saw the woman standing in the children's nursery one day and informed her they were about to close. The docent then realized that the bars at the doorway prevented anyone from entering the room. It is believed that perhaps the ghost is the house's previous owner, Mrs. Juan Girardin, or perhaps Fanny Osbourne Stevenson.

In Big Sur many stories of extraterrestrial spacecraft landings in the Santa Lucia Mountains are told. John Steinbeck described dark watchers, or other beings, in his story "Flight." Robinson Jeffers wrote about them in "Such Counsels You Gave to Me" in the 1930s.

Later, Henry Miller took an interest in these experiences. After all, there are many areas in the Santa Lucia Mountains which, to date, no one but early Indians have seen. Are the "dark watchers" still around? Some say yes, and they came back in 1960s sightings.

Near Mal Paso Creek, Spanish for "bad crossing," a wagon went off the road. Today people hear the bells of the lead horse ringing as they near the creek.

Many people have reported seeing a woman dressed in white, walking the white line in the fog near the Ghost and Witch trees about midnight on the famed 17 Mile Drive in Pebble Beach.

The Macomber House, a huge log home built in Pebble Beach in 1917, sat on top of a hill overlook-

A figure of a woman in white has appeared near the "ghost tree" in Pebble Beach near midnight. Courtesy of the Pat Hathaway Collection.

ing Carmel Beach and Point Lobos. After giving one party and staying only a short time, the Macombers left and for a while, the caretaker lived on the property. The house sat vacant for 40 years. It became known as the ghost house with terror tales told by students who frequented it until it was torn down.

Near the Carmelite Monastery across from Monastery Beach, a transparent lady is said to cross the road at times but no one knows who she might be.

There are stories about a ghost lady in a flowing white gown who frequents the Mission Ranch. Charles Kip Hoebner, son of former owners, never saw her, but his friends did and all descriptions match. Could she be the same ghostly woman who appears in Pebble Beach and near the monastery?

No sightings have been reported at the ranch in recent years, however.

There are reports of the mission bells ringing, but no person has been seen doing it. At the original Carmel Mission in Monterey, the Royal Presidio Chapel, a ghost appears as a priest but has not been identified.

A lovely story about the Franciscan padres is still told today. It is said they spread mustard seed on the paths they walked between the missions. In the spring, the mustard plants bloomed profuse yellow flowers and covered the area. The oil from the seeds was a highly valued seasoning in China and the Chinese in California harvested the seeds, especially in the Salinas Valley area.

Stonepine, Carmel Valley's former Double H working ranch is said to be haunted by the former owner, Ellen Crocker Russell. Employees say she gives everyone a "boot" now and then, which makes them chuckle.

LEGENDS

A Robin Hood of sorts named Juaquin Murietta was, according to some residents, a fictional character created by author John Rollin Ridge. Other people say he was actually a bandit born in 1821 in Mexican Sonora. He was treated poorly by the Americans at a gold mining site and eventually was charged with horse stealing and beaten. He really had been riding his half-brother's horse. To retaliate, Murietta began stealing horses, cattle, and gold and became a real bandit.

According to one account, a poster offering a $1,000 reward for his capture was changed by the bandit to read that he would offer a $5,000 reward. He was shot and killed three years later at the age of 21.

Choctaw Indian Chief Red Eagle came to Carmel in the 1930s. As an orphan, he was adopted by Buffalo Bill Cody and appeared in his shows. He claimed to have seen Jesse James and his brothers killed. He worked with local youths and helped them learn horseback riding and Indian crafts. On special occasions, he appeared in full Indian headress. A Carmel street was named after him but was later changed. He continued to be a colorful figure in Carmel until his death in 1949.

Indian Village, a popular picnic area in Pebble Beach, sits high above the sand dunes in the forest. S.F.B. Morse wrote a description of the area located behind the Cypress Point Club and the Monterey Peninsula Golf Course.

Legend has it that the Ohlone Indians drank spring water there and used the site as a resting place and cure. As a member of the Board of Directors of the Pebble Beach Company, President Gerald Ford dedicated the Village's twenty acres as open space in the Del Monte Forest.

Stagecoach drivers were active in the area east of Carmel as they raced from one location to another. Six-horse coaches came to screeching halts when they arrived at Deacon Howe's in Salinas. Elias Howe had come from Boston and built a post office, inn, and store at the intersection of the road to Monterey. Residents called him "poco loco," a little crazy. That didn't matter to him. He liked good whiskey and word spread that he sold it, too.

Bets were made there and his place became an exciting social spot for stage drivers and passengers.

The coach drivers provided news of scandals, births, deaths and tidbits from Pony Express riders. The coach races provided area ranchers with a way of sustaining themselves when the area had become so arid that farming was impossible.

Charlie Parkhurst was one entirely fearless stagecoach driver who rode the trails to Salinas from southern parts of the county. Parkhurst didn't care whether there were passengers in the coach or not, and raced to Deacon Howe's to be the first one there at any cost, sliding to a stop with dust clouds behind. Later, it was discovered that Parkhurst was actually a woman!

At one time grizzly bears and wolves were prevalent in the area. So one day when James Capen Adams appeared with two bears at the Jolon Rancho near Salinas, people wondered what he was up to. The bears, named Lady Franklin and Ben Washington, wrestled with Adams and he talked to them. He didn't stay very long. After leaving the area, he became known as Grizzly Adams and worked with the P. T. Barnum show in San Francisco. Later, he became a folk hero and a T.V. series was named after him.

By the early 1900s, gathering abalone, those succulent shellfish adored by the Indians, sea otters and George Sterling, was always an excuse for parties. The shellfish can be found at low tide and many people gathered them by moonlight or with lanterns before they became protected marinelife.

Some say that Pop Ernest's cafe on Alvardo Street in Monterey was the place where George Sterling

Pop Ernest, owner of the cafe where George Sterling is said to have written the Abalone Song. Courtesy of the Pat Hathaway Collection.

composed verses over the years for a song called the Abalone Song.

> Oh, some folks boast of quail on toast,
>   Because they think its toney,
> But I'm content to owe my rent,
>   And live on abalone.
> By Carmel Bay, the people say,
>   We feed the lazzaroni
> On Boston beans and fresh sardines
>   And toothsome abalone.
> Some live in hope, and some on dope,
>   And some on alimony

But my tom cat, he lives on fat
    And tender abalone.
Oh! Some drink rain, and some champagne,
    Or brandy by the pony;
But I will try a little rye,
    With a dash of abalone.
The song continues for several verses.

Monterey's deep submarine canyon holds its own mysteries. Sonar picks up unusual sightings such as giant squid and other unidentifiable beings.

Sea creatures with serpent-like characteristics such as huge eyes, humps, and a round head, have been described for over a century by fishermen and sailors on Monterey Bay. One of the creatures, with its long neck and tail, was beached just north of Monterey in 1925. E. L. Wallace, president of the Natural History Society of British Columbia, even ventured to hypothesize that it could have been a plant-eating plesiosaurus which lived in swamps during prehistoric times. Living specimens of coelecanth, primitive marine fishes that scientists said were extinct 70 million years ago, have been found in recent years, too, north of Monterey Bay.

Scientists agree that the moderate temperature and other Monterey Bay characteristics are quite simliar to those at Loch Ness in Scotland. Could Monterey Bay have a Loch Ness legend in its own depths?

VI
Films on the Peninsula

Carmel's natural beauty has drawn filmmakers, like other artists, to the area since 1897 when the first movies, *Hotel Del Monte* and *Surf at Monterey,* two short films, were made. Since then, nearly 200 feature films have been shot on the Monterey Peninsula, as well as innumerable commercials.

In the early years there were few restrictions on filming but as the towns developed, regulations were passed that forced movie production companies to comply. Film production adds to the area's economy: hotels, restaurants, and other service-related businesses prosper during filming. Even so, some towns, including Carmel-by-the-Sea, make it difficult to impossible to film there today.

The movie *Turner and Hootch,* starring Tom Hanks, was almost shot in Carmel but moved to Pacific Grove when there was a change in directors. That was the closest Carmel has come to allowing a feature movie in its town because of traffic and infringement on shops when scenes are filmed in the business district.

MOVIES YOU KNOW

The classic 1934 movie *Treasure Island* starred Wallace Berry and Jackie Cooper. This Metro Goldwyn Mayer production was filmed in Big Sur and Point Lobos and is based on Stevenson's novel, which he wrote as a diversion for his stepson, Lloyd Osbourne. *Rebecca,* which starred Joan Fontaine, George Sanders, and Sir Laurence Olivier was filmed in Carmel in 1940. The United Artist movie was based on the Daphne duMaurier novel.

National Velvet was filmed in Pebble Beach in 1944 and starred Mickey Rooney and Elizabeth Taylor. This was the story of a girl who wins a horse in a raffle and asks Rooney to train it for the Grand National race.

The Graduate, made in 1967 by United Artists and starring Dustin Hoffman and Ann Bancroft, featured scenes at the Bixby Bridge near Big Sur as the famous red Alfa Romeo drove over it. The Academy Award-winning movie was based on the Charles Webb novel about a young man who graduates from college, comes of age, and is seduced by his parents' best friend. *The Sandpiper,* which starred Elizabeth Taylor and Richard Burton, was filmed in Big Sur.

Portions of Universal's family film *Harry and the Hendersons* was filmed in 1987 in the Big Sur redwood forest.

Scenes from *One Eyed Jacks* starring Karl Malden and Marlon Brando were filmed in Pebble Beach.

66

Nearly 200 films have been made in the Carmel area. Here a crew films a scene on the Pebble Beach golf course. Courtesy of the photographer, Kathleen Olson.

Parent Trap with Maureen O'Hara and Brian Keith was also filmed there.

The Templeton Crocker mansion in Pebble Beach was used for the 1975 Disney film, *Escape to Witch Mountain,* which starred Eddie Albert and Ray Milland. The castle was owned by George Stoll, the Academy Award-winning composer and conductor. The Disney movies *The Love Bug* and *Herbie Goes to Monte Carlo,* both featuring a Volkswagen automobile with a mind of its own, were filmed in part there, too. Several scenes in *Star Trek IV: The Voyage Home* were shot on location at the

Monterey Bay Aquarium. The 1992 release *Basic Instinct,* starring Michael Douglas and Sharon Stone, was filmed, in part, at an empty bank building in Carmel Valley. Other scenes were shot along the coast and at a house in the Carmel Highlands and at Big Sur's Garapatta Beach.

Scenes from the 1959 film *A Summer Place* were filmed at the honeymoon cottage at the Mission Ranch.

Blind Date starred Bruce Willis and Kim Basinger and was made in 1987 on the Monterey Peninsula. In 1983, Natalie Wood's final movie, *Brainstorm,*

67

Six years after she starred in *National Velvet,* filmed in the Carmel area, Elizabeth Taylor returns to Pebble Beach on her honeymoon as Mrs. Conrad Hilton, Jr. in 1950. Courtesy of the Pebble Beach Company.

with Cliff Robertson and Christopher Walken was filmed in part in Carmel.

Scenes from two of Clint Eastwood's movies were filmed on the peninsula: *The Eiger Sanction* in 1975, and the 1971 favorite *Play Misty For Me* that Eastwood directed about a Carmel disc jockey who meets a woman on the rebound. The thriller was produced by Robert Daly, now president of Warner Brothers, which releases Eastwood's movies.

THE CELEBRITIES

Errol Flynn, Olivia de Haviland, Greta Garbo, Elizabeth Taylor, Richard Burton, Robert Redford, Mickey Rooney, Marilyn Monroe, Charles Boyer, Montgomery Clift, Burt Lancaster, Clint Eastwood, Kim Novak, Natalie Wood, Lana Turner, Doris Day, Maureen O'Hara, Laurence Olivier, Joan Fontaine, Ronald Reagan, Woody Allen, Mary Pickford, James Stewart, Gene Hackman, Bruce Willis—and even Kermit the Frog—have at one time or another been on location in the area.

The list of celebrities and film-related professionals who live in Carmel is long. Kim Novak lived in Monterey for years and was often seen at the Monterey National Horse Show or at various charitable events. She and her husband recently moved to Oregon.

Beginning in the 1940s actress Jean Arthur lived in Carmel Point for twenty-three years. In the 1940s, Richard Boone started his acting career on the peninsula at the old Del Monte Hotel. He was married to James Hopper's daughter, Jane Hopper, who worked at the *Monterey Peninsula Herald* as a librarian. Phyllis Coats played Lois Lane in the TV

Movie star Kim Novak lived on the Peninsula for many years and was often seen at area benefits. Courtesy of the photographer, Kathleen Olson.

series "The Adventures of Superman" and lived in Carmel for 25 years.

Actress Doris Day is a Carmel Valley resident who with her son, Terry Melcher, is co-owner of the Cypress Inn. Day is active in animals rights and writes a column in the *Carmel Pine Cone* about animals called "Doris's Best Friends." She is often seen at the grocery store with a car filled with her friendly dogs.

Joan Fontaine moved to the Carmel Highlands in the 1980s and is involved in many charitable orga-

nizations. Betty White has a home in Carmel Meadows and is still actively involved in the Morris Animal Foundation. Doug McClure, Dean Stockwell and Merv Griffin have all lived in Carmel Valley at one time or another. Paul Anka and his family lived on Jacks Peak in Monterey for many years before moving to Southern California.

MONTEREY COUNTY FILM COMMISSION

At a 1985 meeting of the Economic Development Commission and the Assembly Committee held at the Monterey City Hall, long-time peninsula resident Clint Eastwood spoke up in favor of promoting filming on the peninsula. He called Los Angeles "jaded" and said the fees imposed there were so high that production companies preferred to film outside the Los Angeles area. He said he'd like to film close to home.

Although he hasn't filmed anything on the peninsula since the 1970s, Eastwood has screened his movies there for local charities such as the Special Olympics, for example, at Carmel's Golden Bough. His Academy Award-winning movie *Unforgiven* premiered at a benefit on August 4, 1992 for the Monterey County Film Commission and Natividad Medical Foundation. Guests wore everything from denim shorts to cocktail outfits for the barbeque and screening. He and several stars (including Gene Hackman) attended the event.

The Monterey County Film Commission was formed in 1986. Filming of both commercials and movie scenes on the peninsula has increased and brought about $3 million in revenue annually to the area.

The Commission's benefit screening of *Dennis the Menace* took place in 1993 after a picnic at the Dennis the Menace Park in Monterey. Creator and cartoonist Hank Ketcham was on hand to greet guests.

FILM FESTIVALS ON THE PENINSULA

The first annual Monterey Independent Film Makers Festival was held in 1968 and 400 people attended. It wasn't until 1985 that plans for a large film festival were made.

Monterey County Supervisor Sam Karas and Morgan Stock, both well known in Monterey Peninsula theater circles, originated the idea of a film festival. They discussed this idea with Alan Weber, the owner of the popular Monterey movie theater, The Dream Theater, and the Monterey County Economic Development Commissioner Joe Cavanaugh. Interest grew and in 1986 a film festival board was formed consisting of several prominent area business leaders.

The four-day 1987 Monterey Film Festival was coordinated by the festival's first Executive Director David Bean, who succeeded in luring La Reina Winery as a major sponsor of the event. This event honored actor Cliff Robertson. It was not a financial success. Although progress was made toward another festival, the first board of directors was displeased with Bean, fired him and subsequently replaced him with two other directors. The most recent was Mikel Pippi, who had previously worked with the Frohman Academy for Children's Drama. Pippi organized the 1988 Monterey Film Festival extravaganza.

The mayor of Deauville, France, Ann d'Ornano, is shown here at the 1988 Monterey Film Festival with actors Clint Eastwood and Jimmy Stewart. Courtesy of the *Carmel Pine Cone.*

Numerous movie stars including Doris Day, Cliff Robertson, Katherine Ross, Sue Langdon, and French Consul General Pierre Vaiaux attended the event. Several hundred guests paid $150 to attend an elaborate black-tie ball and saw Clint Eastwood present James Stewart with a lifetime achievement award. The Mayor of Deauville, France, Anne d'Ornano, also attended the ball. Deauville is the site of the famed annual Cannes Film Festival.

The multi-day event included a luncheon at the Highlands Inn which honored French film director, Roger Vadim, who attended.

Food for the various parties and the ball was flown in from all parts of the country. Sets were designed by professionals. Several seminars were con-

Clint Eastwood was mobbed at the premier of *Unforgiven* in 1992 in Monterey. The premier benefited Natividad Medical Center. Courtesy of the photographer, Kathleen Olson.

ducted featuring Hollywood directors and agents. Foreign movies were shown, including some from Russia, and Russian filmmaker Sergie Oucharon attended the event.

Only five guests appeared at a screening in Salinas of *The Man Who Shot Liberty Vallance* after western star Lee Van Cleef cancelled his appearance. The French composer Maurice Jarre, who wrote the scores for *Dr. Zhivago,* never arrived as promised.

The bills were mounting but both the executive director Mikel Pippi and the board of directors continued to approve expenditures. Pippi was later accused of going on an unlimited spending spree.

Lack of organization and spending beyond limits prevailed throughout every aspect of the event.

Pippi attributed financial losses of $200,000 to low attendance at several screenings and events and a lack of major corporate sponsorships. After the event, while organizers and the Monterey County Supervisors were making excuses to creditors, the board of directors changed several times in an attempt to straighten out the financial chaos.

Generous area businesses were left without payment. Since then, there has been occasional talk but no final decision has been made to ever hold another film festival in the Monterey area.

This lone cypress tree is an identifying symbol for Pebble Beach. Thousands of visitors see the tree each year on the 17 Mile Drive. Courtesy of the Pebble Beach Company.

VII
Pebble Beach

There is no other place like Pebble Beach. Aside from its beauty, social activities, and being known as the golf capitol of the world, Pebble Beach is special for other reasons. Unlike its neighbor Carmel, it is unincorporated, maintains higher standards for development, does not have any form of government, and is owned and managed by the Pebble Beach Company. All of this happened by design.

Pebble Beach was part of two Mexican land grants: Punta de Pinos and El Pescadero. The owner of El Pescadero, Doña Maria del Carmen Barreto, whose family was granted the property in 1836, sold her 4000-acre property to Scotsman David Jacks for about $500 in 1846. She then moved to Monterey where, at the time, there were far more social activities.

Jacks later sold the property to the "Big Four"; Charles Crocker, Mark Hopkins, Collis P. Huntington, and Leland Stanford. These railroad barons owned the Southern Pacific Railroad and the Pacific Improvement Company which had vast landholdings on the Monterey Peninsula.

Pebble Beach's beauty drew travelers who wanted to see the ocean, the ancient Monterey Cypress trees, and travel a forest trail that became known as the famous 17 Mile Drive.

Four- and six-horse carriages took guests from the Hotel Del Monte on a dirt road through Monterey, along Pacific Grove's shoreline, through Pebble Beach along the ocean, past Cypress Point and south to the Carmel Mission. The round trip was close to 35 miles. Along the way, guests stopped at the site which is now the 18th Fairway of the Pebble Beach golf course. They enjoyed picnics and gathered pebbles, thus giving the area the name of Pebble Beach. Tourists could also view herds of buffalo, which freely roamed the property much as deer roam throughout Pebble Beach today.

Another popular stop was Stillwater Cove, adjacent to the current Pebble Beach and Tennis Club. In the 1880s, it was a fishing village and also a place where Chinese and opium were smuggled into California.

THE DUKE

Pebble Beach's open-space lands, golf courses, large residences and large parcels of private land are the result of planning by The Duke of the Del Monte Forest, Samuel Finley Brown Morse, the grandnephew of Samuel Finley Brease Morse, the inventor of the telegraph. Many people thought

"The Big Four." Clockwise, starting upper left: Collis P. Huntington, Mark Hopkins, Leland Stanford, and Charles Crocker. These railroad barons owned the Pacific Improvement Company, which included Pebble Beach, Hotel Del Monte, and Carmel Valley ranchland. Courtesy of the Pebble Beach Company.

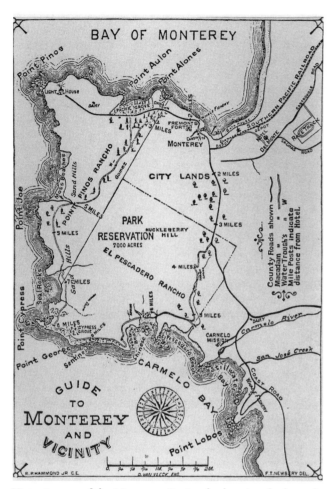

Historic map of the Monterey Peninsula showing the boundaries of the early land grant ranchos. Courtesy of the Pebble Beach Company.

The "Duke of the Del Monte Forest," Samuel Finley Brown Morse. Courtesy of the Pebble Beach Company.

Pebble Beach was Morse's kingdom and he was affectionaly dubbed "The Duke."

Morse attended Andover Preparatory School and graduated from Yale, where he played football. When he first arrived in California, he worked for John Hays Hammond, at his San Joaquin Valley agricultural project. After a year, Morse worked with William Henry Crocker, son of Charles Crocker, on a ranching project in the same valley. Six years later, Morse became manager of the Pacific Improvement Company's property which included Pebble Beach.

Morse was displeased when he saw the original development plans for Pebble Beach, which would have resulted in small lots and houses. He pictured a forest with golf courses and fewer houses. Many people considered him to be a visionary and certainly a man of forethought.

Morse hired Jack Neville to design the Pebble Beach links. In 1912, a series of cottages were built

Guests from the Hotel Del Monte motor through Pebble Beach along the winding drive through cypress and pine forests. Horse-drawn carrriages also traveled what became the 17 Mile Drive. Courtesy of the Pat Hathaway Collection.

that became known as The Lodge. A gate into Carmel was opened in 1913.

In 1915 a gate fee to the Pebble Beach property was established at .25 cents per horse and .50 cents per vehicle. Pebble Beach was enclosed by fences long before anyone in Carmel suggested doing the same thing.

The lodge was destroyed by fire on Christmas Eve in 1917. By 1919, Morse built another lodge which was completed at the same time the golf course was opened.

That same year, Morse founded the Del Monte Properties Company and with the assistance of San Francisco banker, Herbert Fleischhaker, purchased Pebble Beach, the Hotel Del Monte, and other peninsula property owned by the Pacific Improvement Company. Robert Stanton was hired to oversee architectural designs throughout the forest.

LIFESTYLES OF THE FEW

In its early days, Pebble Beach represented a world of social activities for the rich and famous. Morse published a magazine called "Game and Gossip" which described those events. Rumors about frequent guests like Charlie Chaplin, Howard Hughes, and Rudolph Valentino, who was chartering what yacht, and other tidbits, were included in the publication.

Morse believed the peninsula was a youthful place where people wanted to live life rather than watch it go by.

Polo was a major social scene stealer in the 1920s and another excuse for Morse to give parties. Artist Francis McComas and Harry Hunt were frequently seen at Morse's residence.

The Allen Griffin estate on its twenty acres of land was also popular for socializing. Charles Crocker built a home on five acres on Del Ciervo Road called Villa Amici which was popular for parties, too.

There were special evenings of gambling at one select house in Pebble Beach. The Canary Cottage, a yellow building located near the lodge, was used as a casino where guests gambled by invitation only at posh parties. Everyone knew about and participated in the bootlegging which occurred, too, especially at Point Lobos where the spirits were unloaded.

By the early 1950s Pebble Beach road races brought thousands of visitors to watch the excitement. The races were stopped a few years later, however, after one driver was killed. The company was concerned about liability insurance. At the

Polo at Pebble Beach's Collins Field has been a popular sport since the 1920s. Courtesy of the Pebble Beach Company.

Hotel Del Monte, a race track was built for horse and auto racing.

The area grew in popularity. By 1954, the gate fee into Pebble Beach was increased to .75 cents per auto. The inner circle of old-time residents feared the area would become too accessible and overcrowded with "common" people of lesser wealth. The residents sought a way of stratifying those with lots of money from the others. It was decided that golf, because it was an expensive sport, would separate the "haves" from the "have-nots." That's when the Cypress Point Club became the private "in" place to belong and restricted memberships to white people of wealth.

Racial discrimination prevailed; the company did not allow the sale of homes in Pebble Beach to those of Asian, African or Turkish descent. Many

people said Morse created a private kingdom rather like what William Randolph Hearst did with San Simeon. And as recently as the late 1980s, Pebble Beach residents voiced displeasure with the possibility of the Pebble Beach Company's allowing middle-income housing in the area.

Pebble Beach resident Harold Crittenden owned the Templeton Crocker Estate in 1962. He was going to charge admission to his seventeen-room mansion, but promptly changed his mind when the Del Monte Properties Company threatened to evict him from Pebble Beach.

At one time, there was some industry in Pebble

"The Duke" in 1956. Courtesy of the Pebble Beach Company.

The Beach and Tennis Club at Pebble Beach. The location was once the site of a Chinese fishing village at Stillwater Cove. Courtesy of the Pebble Beach Company.

Beach. A sand plant operated there for the Owens Glass Company of Illinois, which used the sand for silicon and ceramicware. One of the largest buyers of sand was the Gallo Vineyards of Modesto. Joseph Gallo owned a Pebble Beach residence and spent time there on occasion. The sand plant was closed in the 1980s after residents protested.

Today, the only industry in Pebble Beach is in the form of retail shops located in the two hotels, golf shops, and golf-course operations.

In 1945, Morse became chairman of the board and his thirty-five-year-old son, John Morse, who was also a Yale graduate, became president of the company.

The state senate honored The Duke in 1965 for his conservation work in providing open space and preserving the natural beauty of Pebble Beach. Upon his death in 1969, Morse left $100,000 to the Robert Louis Stevenson School, where an arts center is named in his honor.

In 1977, the name was changed from the Del Monte Lodge to the Lodge at Pebble Beach. The lodge is a center of social activity for residents. The Tap Room was originally called the Monkey Room for its drawings of monkeys around the walls. It is the most informal of the lodge restaurants, and a gathering place during golf tournaments for players, guests and residents. Its walls are now filled with photos of the famous celebrity golf-tournament players.

Prior to Christmas, a tree-lighting and caroling party is held annually at the lodge where residents and guests gather outdoors for the arrival of Santa Claus and the singing of carols. During Christmas dinners at the lodge, a capella singers entertain in the Cypress Room.

Pebble Beach now boasts two major hotels, the Lodge at Pebble Beach and the Inn at Spanish Bay, and eight golf courses. Pebble Beach, Spyglass, Spanish Bay, the Poppy Hills and nine-hole Peter Hay courses are open to the public. Pro golfer Tom Watson was one of the designers of the Spanish Bay course. Spyglass was designed by Robert Trent Jones in 1966 and has holes named after characters in Stevenson's *Treasure Island*. Monterey Peninsula Country Club's Dunes and Shore courses and the Cypress Point courses are private.

Yachting activities including sailing regattas are popular, and Pebble Beach has its own harbor master and expert sailor, Alan Patterson. His Australian accent is thick and his resemblance to Crocodile Dundee is uncanny. Stillwater Cove is especially active during the summer months and during the AT&T golf tournament.

Stillwater Yacht Harbor. Courtesy of the Pebble Beach Company.

If there is a drawback to living in Pebble Beach, it has to be when residents are driving to the post office or into Carmel behind tourists traveling no more than ten miles per hour as they enjoy every moment of the 17 Mile Drive. But no one complains. It's part of living in what they call paradise.

Pebble Beach is an unincorporated area of the Monterey Peninsula which has been aptly run without city government since its inception. Every now and then, the normally quiet residents do rise up out of their complacency, however, to look beyond their golf swings and become involved in issues.

In 1988, when fire destroyed the Huckleberry Hills area in Pebble Beach, causing millions of dollars in property damage, residents complained that fire assistance was too slow in arriving. The Pebble Beach Fire Department was assisted by other area departments but no one realized the extent of the fire at first.

About forty residents protested at a rally near Bird Rock that same year when the Pebble Beach Company began paving parking areas and destroyed some of the natural landscaping. The issue was brought to the California Coastal Commission and after a few months, the Pebble Beach company was forced to "undo" its improvements and return the area to a natural state, including the dirt parking areas. The company was forced to spray grass seed and recultivate the area that had been destroyed by bulldozing.

In June 1989, residents protested when a prison work crew unknowingly cut down a rare tree, "Eastwood's Golden Fleece," while working on a fire road near the Morse Botanical Garden which contains natural plant habitat.

Pebble Beach is patrolled by private security personnel who carry radios but no weapons. Horseback patrols are also seen on the thirty-five miles of trails that wind along the shore or into the forest among private residences.

OWNERSHIP OF THE PEBBLE BEACH COMPANY

Ownership of Pebble Beach has become complicated in recent years. In the 1970s, 20th Century Fox purchased Pebble Beach. Three years later, oilman Marvin Davis offered to buy 20th Century Fox. He had tried unsuccessfully to purchase baseball teams and the *Denver Post*. Shortly after his

Marvin Davis. Courtesy of the Pebble Beach Company.

offer was made, executive battles at the movie studio occurred, and Davis dropped out only to re-enter the process later.

Davis' bid was accepted and a merger between Fox and Davis' private company was approved. Then Davis, Fox, and the Aetna Corporation joined together to reorganize the Pebble Beach Company. Aetna sold its one-half interest in the Pebble Beach Company to a partnership that included Davis, called Miller, Klutznik, Davis & Gray Company.

In 1984, Davis bought out his other partner at the film studio. A year later Davis and his partners acquired full ownership and control of Pebble Beach.

In 1989, residents heard rumors that the company was being sold to a Japanese firm. Company personnel denied any intention of that sale but it proved to be true. By 1990, Cosmo World, a Japanese-based company, was involved in private negotiations and succeeded in purchasing the Company at a price exceeding $800 million. Within one year, the president of Cosmo World, Minoru Isutani, was dismissed because of his Japanese underworld dealings.

Another era began in Pebble Beach when talk of $700,000 membership fees to the Pebble Beach golf links were discussed by the Japanese ownership. The course had always been open to the public, although with high green fees. Pebble Beach residents were worried that more changes were going to take place.

Then Cosmo World's debt to another Japanese corporation, Mitsubishi, was called in. The debts included ownership of Pebble Beach. There have

Tom Oliver, the President of the Pebble Beach Company, is shown here at the Inn at Spanish Bay. He has presided over the company for more than ten years. Courtesy of the photographer, Kathleen Olson.

been no outwardly noticeable changes to date since Mitsubishi's takeover and the Pebble Beach course remains open to the public.

GOLF

The peninsula is golf country. In its early years even Carmel had a golf course. Pacific Grove, Monterey, and Carmel Valley all have courses, but it's Pebble Beach that is synonymous with golf.

The eighth green at the Pebble Beach Golf Course offers a clear view of the Bay. Courtesy of the Pebble Beach Company.

The first Pebble Beach United States National Amateur Championship Golf Tournament was held in 1929 on the Pebble Beach Golf Course. The winner that year was Harrison R. Johnston. Since that time, tournaments have been a mainstay at the Pebble Beach links.

The Peter Hay course was named after the Del Monte golf professional, Peter Hay, who was hired by Morse in 1919 at the Del Monte Hotel. Later, Hay became golf pro at the Pebble Beach links. Morse named the course after him for his years of dedication. Hay started the Peter Hay Junior Golf tournament which has continued on and off over the years.

Bing Crosby is shown here in a pensive moment. The Crosby tournament and famed clambake actually started in the San Diego area. Courtesy of the Pat Hathaway Collection.

THE CROSBY AND AT&T

Pebble Beach began hosting the Bing Crosby Tournament after Crosby chose to move the event from San Diego County, wherein he invited every type of entertainer to the first party, called the "Clambake." Crosby said he never understood the name because there wasn't a clam in sight.

After World War II, Ted Durein, who was sports editor of the *Monterey Peninsula Herald,* asked if Crosby would be interested in starting a Pebble Beach tournament. After discussion, Crosby agreed, with a purse of $10,000 in prize money. The first

Pebble Beach Crosby Pro-Am tournament was held in 1947.

About 100,000 visitors watch the event each year, which includes a Wednesday celebrity shoot-out and practice rounds. More than ever, the tournament is the best excuse for parties.

Tournament planning begins months ahead as protective fencing goes up around Pebble Beach roads. The security forces are out in great numbers. Most residents don't pick up their mail until late in the day after the crowds leave. (As in Carmel, Pebble Beach has no mail delivery for the houses near the lodge.)

It is almost comical each year when at tournament time, innumerable "for sale" signs go up. Owners hope to lure visitors who may fall in love with the area just as they did. Sometimes it works.

Each year about 1200 volunteers assist with the AT&T golf tournament by selling tickets and acting as marshals to keep the gallery controlled. Tickets allow guests varying degrees of proximity to the activities. Sponsor parties, a brunch by the Pebble Beach Company for a select guest list, and major volunteer parties with entertainment are part of the scene.

The stories surrounding the Crosby tournament are numerous, and always involve celebrities. Over the years, radio legend Phil Harris, who worked on the Jack Benny Show, has been a constant at the tournaments. One year, famed trumpeter Harry James and his pro partner left the 18th tee and were 18 over par. When the scoreboard incorrectly stated 81, Harris, always with outspoken humor, said it didn't matter because by the time the tour-

Clint Eastwood watches a drive at the Crosby. Courtesy of the Pebble Beach Company.

Lou Russo (at right), chairman of the Crosby-AT&T volunteers, is pictured here with his wife Janice and Phil Harris in 1992. Courtesy of Kathleen Olson.

nament was finished, they *would* be 81 over par!

Guests over the years have included Arnold Palmer, Dean Martin, Tom Watson, Jack Nicklaus, Sam Snead, Bob Hope, James Garner, Ben Hogan and Clint Eastwood to name a few. Eastwood said he crashed the first Clambake party in 1952 when he and a friend from Fort Ord claimed they were a writer's assistants. Eastwood said he not only ate the best steak ever but enjoyed the leftover desserts.

Glenn Campbell has become a regular over the years as well. Jack Lemmon is the perennial popular favorite at the tournament, having played in it for 31 years. He still hasn't made the final-day cut. He was given a crystal trophy engraved "To the Golfer with the Most Patience." He maintains a sense of humor and always entertains the gallery. One year, Lemmon had a partner who drank too much. The partner fell a few times and every now and then Lemmon said he heard bells. He didn't find out until later that his partner's coat was lined with clanking pint bottles.

Bob Hope, who worked with Crosby for years, said Crosby's swing was so slow that everyone would study their clubs or the labels while he was in a back swing.

In the 1980s the Crosby family, namely Kathryn Crosby, widow of Bing Crosby, decided not to continue the golf tournament under the Crosby name. The Pebble Beach Company solicited AT&T as the tournament sponsor and the first golf tournament in Pebble Beach under the AT&T name began in 1986.

The celebrities come and go but one thing remains constant: the weather. The tournament is

Bob Hope clowns in front of the gallery at an early Crosby. Courtesy of the Pat Hathaway Collection.

In 1975, the Pebble Beach Foundation was formed to handle charitable activities involving the proceeds from the tournament. Gerald Ford was named to the Pebble Beach Company's Board of Directors. In 1992, Pebble Beach hosted the premier golfing event, the Professional Golf Association's Open Tournament, along with the AT&T and the Spaulding. Proceeds from the tournaments are divided among area youth organizations. Pebble Beach will host the 100th PGA Open again in the year 2000.

ROBERT LOUIS STEVENSON SCHOOL

The Robert Louis Stevenson School in Pebble Beach, a college preparatory school, was founded in 1952 by Robert and Marian Ricklefs as a boys' boarding school. It became the Douglas School and then the Del Monte School for Boys before it became known as the Robert Louis Stevenson School in 1954, with eighteen students. Within one year, it grew to an enrollment of twenty-eight students.

There is a close bond between the school and S.F.B. Morse and the Del Monte Properties Company, which donated ten acres to the school as an athletic field, the first of many gifts to the school over the years. Rivalry exists between Stevenson and Carmel High School in most athletic events.

Later the company deeded the land which was to become the Erdman Memorial Chapel, used for community and school services.

During the 1970s, women were admitted to the school as day students. Now the school has 50 acres of land and an enrollment of more than 400, including day students and coed boarders. The

played during the first week of February. Rain comes down, the wind picks up, umbrellas come out on the course, and everyone sighs. In 1991, the tournament could not be completed because the storms were so bad.

Several politicians, including former president Gerald Ford, are regulars in the tournament. Former vice president Dan Quayle has played in the tournament also. In 1993, comedian Bill Murray dragged a bystander and longtime peninsula resident, Rody Holt, into the sand where she promptly fell, all in good fun. Actor Michael Keaton of *Batman* fame and Marvin Davis were partners in 1990.

Once known as the Douglas Boys School, the Robert Louis Stevenson School is Pebble Beach's prestigious co-ed prep school. Courtesy of the Robert Louis Stevenson School.

Famed tenor Luciano Pavarotti performed at a Robert Louis Stevenson School benefit in 1991. He is shown here with Laurie Hall, Diane Trabert, Jill Vogel, and Tibor Rudas. Courtesy of the Robert Louis Stevenson School.

school has its own radio station, KSPB. The school boasts that 100 percent of its students go on to four-year colleges and universities. Since 1983, Joe Wandke has served as the progressive headmaster.

Many of the students are sons and daughters of celebrities including Ryan O'Neal, Paul Anka and Clint Eastwood. The Board of Trustees has included such notable celebrities names as Efrem Zimbalist III, Davis Factor, and the heads of many corporations.

The school is like other preparatory schools when its students decide to play pranks. In 1985, the seniors painted the bridge that crosses a portion of the school's campus a bright pink. Then they brought in sand and made a beach with a canoe and beach chairs.

Recently, the school purchased Carmel's Briarcliff Academy as a K-12 school for about 165 students on two campus locations.

Elaborate fundraising events have included a concert in 1991 featuring the opera singer Luciano Pavarotti.

VIII
Social Events

The peninsula has been filled with social events of every variety since its early history—including baseball.

ABALONE LEAGUE

The 1920s saw the formation of Carmel's Abalone League, founded in 1921 by playwright Charles Van Riper. An oversized baseball was used during their games on Sunday afternoons at the Carmel Point field. The league was named "abalone" because a home run meant the ball flew toward the sea and down the rocks with the abalone. The games were later moved to a field in the Carmel woods near the middle school on Rio Road.

Mrs. Alice Josselyn, the mother of two writers, stuffed newspapers into the field's gopher holes, but injuries occurred anyway. The league's crutches were kept at Doc Staniford's Drug Store on Ocean Avenue and San Carlos Street, operated by Dr. J. E. Beck. The league raised money by holding stage plays at the Arts and Crafts Theater.

Winners took home the Abalone Cup, which was really the top off the *Monterey Peninsula Herald*'s stove. No one ever knew it until later when the *Herald* editor unsuccessfully tried to have the award named the Herald Cup. The 1923 winner was

Harrison Godwin, co-owner of the La Playa Hotel.

The very first softball decision in history was handed down by Judge Kenesan Mountain Landis, a United States baseball commissioner, regarding an argument between a Carmel player and umpire. The results, however, are lost to history.

Every team had two women players and each team had a unique name like the Shamrocks or Pirates. Edward Kuster, James Hopper, cartoonist R. C. Smith, artist Jo Mora, S.F.B. Morse and Robert and Virginia Stanton played occasionally. Game results were printed in the *Carmelite* or *Carmel Sun* newspapers.

In 1921, writer Fred Bechdolt and Edward Kuster tried to organize a Carmel Country Club, which would have included tennis but not golf, on a site at Ocean Avenue and Junipero Street. There wasn't enough interest and the site eventually became the location for the Carmel Presbyterian Church.

Elite guests often visited Pebble Beach's Cypress Point Club parties where they were entertained by prominent area residents like the Harold Mack family, whose residence became the private Santa Catalina Girls School in Monterey. Somerset Maugham and Coco Chanel were guests at the

Carmel's Abalone League was the first softball league in the western United States. Courtesy of the Local History Department, Harrison Memorial Library.

Elins' Monterey home. The Sidney Fishes gave immense parties with guest lists including the names of George Gershwin and Charles Lindberg.

In the 1960s the hottest action in Carmel was a domino clinic at the La Playa Hotel under Bud Allen's ownership. It was Allen who started the "Hookers Ball" at the Mission Ranch as a benefit for Carmel's schools. Men and women dressed for the part with Merv and Nancie Sutton, owners of Nielsen's Market, receiving rave reviews for their costumes in 1989.

In the 1970s, Clint Eastwood hosted celebrity tennis tournaments at the Beach and Tennis Club in Pebble Beach with such stars as Jonathan Winters, who entertained large audiences attending the event.

PENINSULA PARTIES

The Peninsula has a complete array of social events from large festivals such as The Great Monterey Squid Festival, benefits like The Great Mon-

Merv and Nancie Sutton pose at the 1989 annual Hookers Ball. The ball was held at the Mission Ranch as a benefit for Carmel schools. Courtesy of the *Carmel Pine Cone*.

terey County Pigeon Race, a Hunt Luncheon during the Pebble Beach Jumper Derby, and the SPCA Auxilliary Fashion Show, to the classy and world famous Concours d'Elegance held at the 18th green on the Pebble Beach links.

One of the most welcomed guests at every social event is the *Monterey Peninsula Herald*'s social columnist, Margye Neswitz, who was previously the social editor of the *Carmel Pine Cone*. She succeeded Ann Germain at the *Herald*.

Neswitz appears on a weekly TV show for the local NBC affiliate KSBW-TV where she inter-

Composer Morton Gould enjoys his 75th birthday party in 1989 with *Monterey Peninsula Herald* society columnist Margye Neswitz. Courtesy of Philip Neswitz.

The annual sand castle contest began on Carmel Beach in 1962. It is sponsored by the American Institute of Architects and brings more than 400 entrants to the beach every year. Courtesy of the *Carmel Pine Cone.*

views celebrities and tells viewers about coming events. Neswitz and her husband Philip moved to Pebble Beach after spending years in Chicago and New York.

On any given weekend the peninsula might have as many as thirteen social events for her to cover. Following the October 17, 1989 earthquake that destroyed so much property in Monterey County, Clint Eastwood gathered other celebrities, including comedian Chevy Chase, for a benefit dinner to help earthquake victims in the county. About 1000 people attended the event. Other events include the annual Fourth of July bash at the Pebble Beach and Tennis Club; the Crystal Ball in 1989 for the Monterey County Hospice with its white-flocked Christmas trees brought out hundreds of party-goers; and a Hollywood Spectacular party in 1992 that featured entertainer Rita Coolidge in a benefit for the Suicide Prevention and Crisis Center.

Each year Laguna Seca Raceway hosts the annual Historic Auto Races among its other car races, at-

tracting famed drivers like Mario Andretti and Rick Mears.

The first Carmel-by-the-Sea annual Sand Castle Contest began in 1962 and is now sponsored by the American Institute of Architects. This event brings about 400 entries to Carmel's beach for judging.

The hostess with the Peninsula's beat is Artie Early. Monterey's reputation as a social town has given Early many opportunities to host some of the most popular parties and chair several of the area's most successful events.

Early and her husband, Lee, have lived in a large two-story Monterey colonial since 1975. Martha Stewart, Barclay Ferguson, James Villis, Craig Claiborne, Jean Philip Cousteau and numerous sport celebrities and movie stars have been Early's guests.

She is best known for two special events on the peninsula: Tablescapes and the Gourmet Gala. Tablescapes is a protected trademark for the event that offers displays of outstanding and unique table

Tab Hunter appeared as a celebrity chef with Gourmet Gala founder Artie Early. The gala benefits the March of Dimes. Courtesy of Artie Early.

Artist Salvador Dali was a frequent visitor to Pebble Beach, and once appeared at the Bal Masque fundraiser reclined on a bed. Courtesy of the Pebble Beach Company.

settings as a Hospice benefit. Professional interior designer Ann Anka, Tiffany and Company, and Dolores Hope have created wonderful settings at this event in past years, but the event is no longer being held.

One of the peninsula's most complicated events is the tour de force called the Gourmet Gala, which Early began in 1986 for the March of Dimes. Celebrity chefs prepare food for hundreds of guests to sample. James Brolin, Brooke Shields, Tab Hunter, and Clint Eastwood, who prepared his special spaghetti western dinner, have participated. It has been quite a task to coordinate the celebrity chefs, the travel arrangements, the kitchen set-ups, along with the normal party planning activities.

Two other popular area hostesses are Virginia Stanton and Jane Dart. Dart, a former actress who once played opposite Gary Cooper, came to Pebble Beach with her husband, Justin. The Dart family is known for their philanthropy in the arts.

Stanton and her husband, Robert, came to the area in 1920 and have given spectacular parties over the years. She recalled one during a Crosby Clambake when Bing Crosby asked her for a glass. She automatically handed him a Baccarat stem crystal—which he promptly dropped.

Her husband, Robert, helped decorate Salvador Dali's bed which was used at a fundraising ball for artists in the 1950s. Dali and his wife reclined on the bed during the event.

Philanthropist Virginia Stanton has assisted many organizations over the years. Courtesy of Kathleen Olson.

The Stantons first lived in Pebble Beach and then moved to Carmel Valley. During wartime, the Stantons still entertained but gave spaghetti parties instead of more elaborate ones. She also recalled many beach parties and calls Carmel a theater town.

Bob and Dolores Hope, friends of the Stantons, appeared at the 1992 opening of the Stanton Center, the Maritime Museum and History Center at Monterey's Custom House Plaza to which Virginia Stanton donated $1 million. On August 6, 1993, her friends hosted a gala 90th birthday party for Virginia Stanton.

The six-day Masters of Food and Wine event takes place each year at the Carmel Highlands Inn and features such gourmet chefs as Jacques Pepin, Paul Bocuse, and Julia Child, who celebrated her 80th birthday at the inn on October 12, 1992. About 1200 gourmet aficionados and wine connoisseurs attend this event annually, which includes an opening night tasting and several special dinners.

Equestrian activities have continued at the Pebble Beach Equestrian Center, where polo matches were held on the adjacent Collins Field until 1989. The Monterey National Horse Show has drawn thousands of spectators for more than 50 years. The show is a combination of Western and English competition with a high-stakes Grand Prix and black-tie event.

The prestigious Del Monte Kennel Club Show is featured at the Lodge each year and takes place on the 18th green of the Pebble Beach course. Internationally known judges and Carmel residents, Joe Tacker and Derek Rayne, have chosen the Best in Show at this event. Rayne, who has judged in 27 countries around the world, is the Club's permanent honorary president and is also referred to as the King of Judges. He has owned and operated his popular clothing shop in Carmel for many years.

Vintage automobiles of immense value are on display annually at the Concours d'Elegance, on the 18th green at Pebble Beach. Celebrities include television personality and car collector Jay Leno, novelist Sydney Sheldon, fashion designer Ralph Lauren, and author Clive Cussler.

Ferraris, Dusenbergs, Mercedes, Jaguars, and others worth millions of dollars are under the scrutiny of spectators and judges. Christies of New York holds an auction in Monterey following the

Above: a horse and rider
clear an obstacle at the
Pebble Beach Jumper Derby.
Courtesy of the photographer,
Kathleen Olson.

Left: honorary President of
the Del Monte Kennel Club
Derek Rayne judges dog
shows around the world.
Courtesy of Derek Rayne.

The Pebble Beach Concours d'Elegance draws guests and exotic cars from around the world, including historic auto collector and Tonight Show host Jay Leno. Photo at left courtesy of the Pebble Beach Company; Leno photo courtesy of the photographer, Will Wallace. Airegin Images.

event. Cartoonist Eldon Dedini's posters for these events have become popular collector's items.

The Monterey Bay Aquarium gained international acclaim for its magnificent marine life exhibits, but it is also host to many society parties. Prince Philip of England was the honored guest at a benefit dinner for the World Wildlife Fund. Philanthropist David Packard, founder of the aquarium, and his daughter, Julie Packard, greeted guests personally that night in 1991. The first anniversary party of the Monterey Bay Sanctuary was held at the aquarium in 1993. The Bach Festival uses the facility to host a dinner there. Other events held at the aquarium include a Taste of Monterey and parties for the Monterey Jazz Festival.

Many members of royalty have visited the Pebble Beach area over the years, including King Juan Carlos of Spain who visited in 1987. Britain's Prince Andrew visited in 1989 and attended equestrian activities at the Pebble Beach Equestrian Center.

The opening of the Inn at Spanish Bay was celebrated when owner Marvin Davis and his wife, Barbara, hosted a spectacular celebrity-packed party at the hotel at a cost of over $1 million. Sydney Poitier and Clint Eastwood were two of the star guests who attended the event. About 1000 personally invited guests of the Davises attended.

For the opening, each of the inn's various dining rooms were decorated in different themes, including an Italian room featuring various pasta dishes, a Spanish room with tapas, and a seafood room complete with a 20-foot-long ice sculpture of a mermaid in a large shell. There was also a room decorated with a complete chocolate landscape set on a large conference table.

The Monterey Jazz Festival is now in its 36th year. In 1957, Jimmy Lyons, a former radio disc jockey in Southern California who produced the armed forces radio show in the 1940s called "Jubilee," organized the first festival. The first

93

In this photo titled "The Final Hug" Monterey Jazz Festival Founder Jimmy Lyons is embraced by Dizzy Gillespie at the 1992 festival. Lyons died in April 1994. Courtesy of Will Wallace. Airegin Images.

planning session for the event took place at the original Doc Rickett's lab, the place where Steinbeck's friend worked in Pacific Grove.

On September 18, 1992, a tribute was given to Lyons when he announced he was retiring from the festival. This event, held at the Monterey County Fairgrounds, attracts about 7,000 people each year.

Jake Stock and the Abalone Stompers were featured at the first Festival in 1958 along with Dave Brubeck and Dizzy Gillespie, one of the most popular entertainers. Gillespie thought the festival was unique because everyone felt they were a real part of the festival and not just bystanders.

In addition to Gillespie, Louis Armstrong, Quincy Jones, Billy Eckstine, Herbie Mann, Miles Davis and Branford Marsalis have performed there.

Among other important musical events is the popular Bach Festival, founded in 1935 by Dene Denny and Hazel Watrous. Performances take place at the Carmel Sunset Center and several other area locations for a two-week period in July.

Another musical group, The Carmel Music Society, has brought the great musical talent of Isaac Stern, Vladimir Horowitz, Igor Stravinsky, Jan Peerce and the Vienna Boys Choir to the Sunset Center also.

The Monterey County Symphony was formed after World War II. The musicians number 72 and come from all parts of the country to perform with the orchestra during its regular concert season.

One large symphony party took place at the Dennis LeVett residence in Pebble Beach to celebrate composer Morton Gould's birthday in 1989. Guests dined outdoors under a huge tent. During dessert, when miniature white chocolate grand pianos filled with raspberries and chocolate mousse were being served, a violent rainstorm kicked up and blew the tent so severely that the party was interrupted. Although most guests found it disconcerting, one 84-year old woman, Marguerite MacLaughlin, said it was the only exciting part of the evening.

Carmel's Scottish population is quite extensive. David Jacks, poet George Sterling, Robert Louis Stevenson, and Salinas resident William Hartnell, were all of Scottish descent. Each year the Scottish Society holds a formal Tartan Ball, and annual highland games and festivals are held at the Monterey County Fairgrounds.

Since 1970, Monterey has hosted a Parade of Nations, thirteen weeks of festivals to celebrate ethnic heritage and further understanding among ethnic groups. Ambassadors and other government officials attend the events.

Pacific Grove also has several festival celebrations. The historic Festival of Lanterns began in 1880 during the last week of July. It began around an oriental legend about a Mandarin's daughter who was forbidden to marry her sweetheart, and who later drowned herself. Chinese and Japanese fishing boats were lit with lanterns on the bay in her memory. Since then Pacific Grove residents place lanterns in their windows during the festival. Fireworks, a boat parade and the crowning of a queen is also part of the festivities.

The annual Big Sur marathon begins in town and continues on its 26-mile route on Highway One to Carmel. Tens of thousands of runners from around the world trace its course up the coast.

The Monarch Butterfly Festival and Parade have been held each October for nearly 50 years. Children especially enjoy the festivities, including the parade in which they usually dress as butterflies with wings and antennae.

The annual Great Monterey Squid Festival, and the Strawberry, Garlic and Artichoke festivals all draw thousands of visitors annually to the peninsula. The variety of events is endless.

IX
The Chinese Heritage

The influence and history of the Chinese in Carmel is immense. From Monterey south to Point Lobos, the Chinese developed their distinct culture, and made their mark in the fishing industry.

The Chinese came to the area in the 1860s to work for the Southern Pacific Railroad or the Pacific Improvement Company. Others worked in the mines during the gold rush. Many Chinese who emigrated to California from the Kwangtung Province chose to settle in the Salinas and Pajaro Valleys because of similarities in the environment to their homeland.

The first Chinese resident in Monterey was from Macao, and named Annam. He worked for the Alta California governor, Pablo Vicente Sola and was given the Spanish name of Antonio Maria de Jesus.

The Chinese people lived on their boats and sailed to the Monterey area knowing gold when they saw it and knowing how to fish. As the Indian population dwindled, the Chinese population grew larger. The Chinese Village, which was erected above Stillwater Cove, became a tourist stop for Hotel Del Monte guests along the 17 Mile Drive. Tourists along the 17 Mile Drive also enjoyed seeing the lanterns in the fishing boats.

In May of 1882, the Chinese Exclusion Act was passed which forbade Chinese immigrants from coming into the United States. The Chinese thereupon began using aliases to avoid any conflict with the government. By becoming a Catholic, using a Spanish name and learning the Spanish language, anyone could become a "gente de razon" or person of reason. Thus, Spaniards could be Indians, Africans, or Chinese, as well as Spanish, and there were many Chinese Spaniards with Spanish names.

The Chinese farmed and dried abalone, and Point Lobos became a popular place for their fishing enterprise. In the 1870s the shells were collected for furniture inlays and jewelry. The Chinese harvested kelp and occasionally shot male sea lions for body parts which they used for aphrodesiacs. They also ate sea urchins and squid; it appeared that they used everything the sea could provide.

Carmel was a popular fishing spot as was Pebble Beach at Pescadero Point where a fishing village was established. Whalers Cove at Point Lobos was the most significant village, but by the late 1870s the Chinese left Point Lobos, which had become a bootlegging area for smugglers to offload their goods such as illegal Chinese immigrants. This was especially true after the Exclusion Act. Stillwater

Jung family shell stand at Pebble Beach, ca. 1890. Courtesy of the Pebble Beach Company.

Cove was the site of a smuggling incident as well when a ship named the *Halcyon* brought a band of Chinese onto shore.

Anti-Chinese activities began in the 1870s. The Workingman's Party and the Order of Caucasians took active roles in decrying the presence of the Chinese. Where the importance of Chinese labor was essential to agriculture, there was little, if any, disputing their presence. Monterey had few problems with the Chinese because it already had such a thorough mix of ethnic groups including Spanish, Mexican, Portuguese, Chinese, and Italian residents. Among other things, Chinatown in Monterey was infamous for opium, prostitution and gambling.

In 1876 a Chinese man named Go Ti wanted to open a house of prostitution in Monterey, but the Chinese leader Tim Wong and others refused his request. Later, Wong was found hanging from a tree. By 1900 there were more than 150 Chinese living in their village at Point Alones. But the end was near.

Whalers Cove, pictured here in 1906, was a popular fishing area for the Chinese. Courtesy of the Point Lobos State Reserve Collection. Pat Hathaway Collection.

In 1905, because residents complained about the terrible odor from drying squid and fish, the Chinese were forbidden to continue their work. At the same time, Pacific Grove no longer wanted the Chinese in its town. In 1905, the Pacific Improvement Company refused to renew the Chinese leases. After the 1906 earthquake, however, not only did more artists come to the area, but more Chinese from San Francisco as well.

With the influx of additional Chinese into the Village, it appeared that the population was there to stay.

After three previous fires, a 1906 fire destroyed all but 16 of the 100 buildings at the village, although no one was injured or killed. Some said the Pacific Improvement Company set the fire when it began to evict the Chinese. The move appeared to be a political power play. The company offered alternative sites for the Chinese at McAbee Beach, and began advertising that the Point Alones beach area was, once again, open for sunbathers. From that point on, fewer Chinese remained on the peninsula and little of their culture remains today.

The Hopkins Marine Center in Pacific Grove is now located on the site of a Chinese graveyard and the old fishing village.

X

Surrounding Areas

Carmel is not an island, although it tries to be on occasion. Each of the neighboring communities has many things in common, and yet each maintains its own definite persona.

CARMEL HIGHLANDS

Ten miles south of Monterey, or a day's ride by horse and buggy, and directly south of Carmel, lies an expanse of land called the Carmel Highlands. This area, located high above the Pacific Ocean, was a place where, in the 1900s, sailors from Scotland often jumped ship and settled. It was also an area where coal and lime were mined.

The area was already home to many Scottish families when James Franklin Devendorf built his Highlands Inn. The road was nearly impassable and a challenge in itself; Devendorf speculated that a new planned highway would increase his business from San Luis Obispo to Monterey. Today it is an area of large ocean-front homes.

SALINAS

The Salinas Valley, often called the Valley of the Nile because of its highly productive farms, varies in width from 10-20 miles and features the Salinas River, the third longest in California and the long-est underground river in the United States.

In 1795, more than 8000 acres were granted to Jose Maria Soberanes and his father-in-law Joaquin Castro and was called the Buena Vista Rancho. When the Mexican land grants were divided, William E. P. Hartnell, another Scotsman, was one of the first to obtain a grant, claiming 50,000 acres of land. He became the British vice consul in Monterey. Hartnell College in Salinas was named in his honor.

In the 1920s Salinas became an agricultural leader for peas, strawberries and lettuce. Barley, corn, broccoli, artichokes, and sugar beets were also harvested. The first crop of lettuce in Monterey County was produced by Orrin O. Eaton in 1917.

Claus Spreckles, a German, built the world's largest sugar refinery in 1897 at a cost of nearly $3 million. A tavern owned by Spreckles called the Louvre was frequented by plant workers until their wives objected.

Rubber from a desert shrub called Guayule was made by the Intercontinental Rubber Company in Salinas during World War II. Mining was popular and areas south of Salinas near King City are rich in oil.

Salinas has allowed greater residential and busi-

Philanthropist David Packard, actor Douglas Fairbanks, Jr., and Stanford University President Donald Kennedy attend the Hopkins Marine Library dedication in 1990. Courtesy of Philip Neswitz and the *Carmel Pine Cone*.

ness expansion than any other area in Monterey County.

PACIFIC GROVE

This town is more famous for its Monarch butterflies than anything else. The butterflies are protected by a city ordinance enacted on November 16, 1938, when a $500 fine was imposed on anyone caught molesting butterflies. The fine has grown to $1,000 today.

More than 100 years ago, Pacific Grove was formed as a Christian retreat after hundreds of Methodists met one summer on the shore at Lovers Point. Their Methodist-style prohibition was in full swing after that point.

In 1883, the town's rules prohibited gambling, drinking, dancing, profanity, fast buggy driving, firearms, and smoking. The retreat was enclosed by a fence with a locked gate and a strict curfew required that anyone under the age of eighteen had to be inside by 8:00 p.m. For nearly 10 years there were no arrests for violation of the rules.

Eventually people rebelled against the strict regulations. A few residents built a dance hall on the northern edge of town, called New Monterey, and card games were popular in the back of Hollenbeck's Cigar Store. More rebellious citizens rocked the electric trolley off its tracks and headed for the nearby saloon to get a drink while the trolley was being set straight again. In the 1930s Judge Benjamin Langford, who owned a house within the retreat gates, chopped down the gate one night after tiring of asking for the key. The gate was never replaced.

Early residents included R. L. Holman, who founded Holman's Store. The town has worked hard to preserve many historical buildings and many large Victorian homes have been converted to popular bed and breakfast inns. The Point Pinos Lighthouse on the Pacific Grove shore opened in 1855. The second floor contains a bedroom decorated from the period of 1893–1914 when Emily A. Fish was the lighthouse keeper.

Pacific Grove is home to the Asilomar Conference Center, which was founded in 1913 for the YWCA. ("Asilomar" means a retreat by the sea.) Phoebe Apperson Hearst, mother of William Randolph Hearst, made major contributions to its development. Architect Julia Morgan, who had worked on projects for Mrs. Hearst, planned the site. Originally a group of YWCA women pitched tents on the beach site. Over the years major conferences have been held there. In 1956, the center was purchased by the California State Parks Department and continues to maintain its non-profit status.

The main building at the exclusive Stonepine resort in Carmel Valley is part of what was once the Double H working thorough-bred ranch. Courtesy of Daniel Barduzzi and Stonepine.

CARMEL VALLEY

When it comes to ranch land and pick-up trucks, Carmel Valley reigns supreme. Besides ranches, the area also contains resorts such as Quail Lodge and Stonepine, golf courses, and expensive residences.

The first school in the entire Carmel area was called the Carmelo School and founded by James Meadows. He came to the area in 1837 as a British sailor who hid away and was later arrested. When granted his freedom, he married a member of the Peralta family, which had large land holdings.

Carmel Valley was once a ranchers' and hunters' haven, but modern developments like the Carmel Valley Ranch resort, Rancho Canada and Carmel Valley Golf and Country Clubs changed all that.

Three popular senior retirement developments are in the Valley; Hacienda Carmel, Del Mesa and the Carmel Valley Manor attract those looking for a simpler lifestyle.

For an area that was once owned entirely by the Spanish and Mexican governments, it's ironic that in 1992 the Immigration and Naturalization Service made some spectacular raids in Carmel Valley to catch illegal aliens from Mexico.

Former United States Congressman Leon Panetta and Doris Day live in Carmel Valley. General James Doolittle lived there until his death in 1993.

The upper valley has its own water company, Cachagua Mutual Water Company. Several wineries including Carmel Valley's Chateau Julien provide popular local vintages. Franciscan priests at the Soledad Mission are credited with planting wine grapes there in the 1770s, but the vines were lost through time. It wasn't until the 1960s that Monterey County became recognized as an important wine producing area.

Since 1967, a large Zen Buddhist center has been located in the valley's Tasajara Hot Springs area. In 1904 a hotel was located there with bath houses but it was totally destroyed by fire in 1949. The Zen Center of San Francisco purchased the property and it has been headquarters for Zen study since that time.

Stonepine is a very private and exclusive executive resort. Originally it was the Double H, a working horse ranch owned by the Henry Potter Russell family. Mrs. Russell was the daughter of one of the Crocker family members. Russell founded the California Thoroughbred Breeders Association, and Santa Anita Race Track in Southern California named a race after him.

Stonepine is a retreat for many celebrities like former San Francisco 49er quarterback Joe Montana and actress Michele Lee and her family.

The Double H and its elaborate equestrian center, built by Russell in 1930, was home to about 200 fine race horses including the famed Majestic Prince. Today this ranch is surrounded by national forest land and special benefit parties with the "Great Gatsby" and "Gone with the Wind" themes are held there.

MONTEREY

This city was the first white North American settlement on the Pacific Coast and California's first capitol. California's first newspaper, *The Californian,* was started there in 1846 by Dr. Robert Baylor Semple and William Colton. The first brick house was built there in 1848 on Decatur Street and became the location for California's first hotel, The Washington.

During its early history, Monterey was heavily influenced by the Mexicans. Its old adobe dwellings, like Casa de Soto, the Larkin House, Casa Sobrantes, and Casa Abrego gave the town an aura of antiquity. It became known as the Old Capitol. By the 1850s the magical draw of Monterey's harbor was losing prestige to the newer San Francisco Bay.

Monterey relied on its sardine and salmon fishing industry for its livelihood. The F. E. Booth Cannery was the first canning factory. Steinbeck wrote of the area in his book *Cannery Row.* In the 1930s and 40s, vast numbers of fish were processed by the canneries. Squid and anchovies have been the fishing industry's most reliable mainstays. Even now, with the area containing a designated sanctuary, commercial fishing will continue to be a significant industry on the bay.

Fisherman's Wharf was built in 1946 for boats to unload their giant cargos of fish. For a while, the whaling industry dominated the pier, but the sardine industry became Monterey's leader. The old pier now houses shops and restaurants, the commercial fleet having moved to the Municipal Wharf.

Monterey's Presidio is one of the country's oldest military establishments. Originally, military life was centered around an adobe building there called a cuartel. The United States Defense Language Institute is located there now.

The Bixby Bridge on Highway One takes travelers south to Big Sur. It is shown here under construction in 1932. Courtesy of the Pat Hathaway Collection.

Monterey also incorporates the United States Naval Post Graduate School, which was the former site of the old Hotel Del Monte, Fort Ord, which is now scheduled to close, and the Monterey Institute of International Studies. Monterey, as well as Seaside and Marina, have relied heavily on the military to support their economy. The effects of Fort Ord's closing are yet to be felt. Discussions are taking place to decide what to do with that mil-

itary base. Ideas range from a four-year university to the site of a long-discussed performing arts center and a shopping center.

A humorous invasion has haunted Monterey. In 1842, Commodore Thomas Catesby Jones thought war had been declared between the United States and Mexico. He sent men ashore at Monterey Bay and raised the American Flag, holding it at bay for 30 hours.

Realizing his giant error, the Mexican flag was flown and a salute of apology was fired. Four years later, however, the city was taken by Commodore John D. Sloat. Jones eventually returned to command the United States Pacific Squadron. A Commodore Jones Society was founded in 1965 and meets regulary to discuss Monterey history.

AWESOME BIG SUR

This area of lost treasures and rugged coastline seems immune to the modern world. The actual town of Big Sur is surrounded by redwood forests. Fog is common and the temperature is mild. There are lovely coves in Big Sur including Jade Cove where nephrite jade is often found by visitors.

The Pfeiffer family moved to Big Sur in 1869. Barbara Pfeiffer started the first school in their own house. Sam Trotter and Adelaide Pfeiffer married, had five children and settled near the Palo Colorado River area.

In the 1870s, the Partington, Castro, Post, Trotter and Harlan families arrived. The Harlans made it quite clear that they didn't live in Big Sur, they lived in Lucia, to the south. It was William Brainard Post who started the first Big Sur post office. Charles Bixby came in 1868 and settled at what is now Bixby Creek, formerly Mill Creek, 18 miles south of Carmel. His father supervised the building of a road from the Carmel Mission to Big Sur. The 342-foot Bixby Bridge is famous for being the longest reinforced concrete archway in the west.

Andrew Molera State Park was named for the son of pioneer Eusebius Molera, who brought buffalo to Big Sur.

Rancho El Sur, the glorious stretch of land that overlooks the Pacific, was once the center of Big Sur's social activities. Juan Cooper's son, John Bautista Henry Cooper, built an outdoor dance floor at the ranch where families gathered often.

Dr. John Roberts was the Pennsylvania physician who is credited with persuading the government to build Highway One, which opened in 1937. Everyone assumed that the highway was being built as a private road for Hearst's San Simeon castle.

Big Sur is not immune from natural catastrophe. In the 1970s a fire destroyed nearly 4,000 acres in the Ventanna Wilderness and the Andrew Molera State Park. Mudslides and rockslides have from time to time closed the roads. And another huge fire in 1977 burned for three weeks and destroyed nearly 100,000 acres of land.

Big Sur gained a reputation for harboring drug lords and unconventional lifestyles such as communes during the 1960s. Occasionally the police still find large acreage filled with marijuana plants.

In 1962, Stanford University graduates Michael Murphy and Richard Price founded the Esalen Institute. About 10,000 people each year attend sessions there on spiritual and mind-body enlightenment.

This interior shot of John Steinbeck's cottage in Pacific Grove shows the desk where he worked as well as other memorabilia. Courtesy of the John Steinbeck Arthurian Society.

CALIFORNIA

This 1929 program cover for the 33rd National Amateur Golf Championship conveys the spectacular natural

THIRTY THIRD
**National Amateur
Golf Championship**
PEBBLE BEACH
CALIFORNIA
1929

DEL MONTE

setting that has drawn golfers to Pebble Beach for nearly a century. Courtesy of the Pebble Beach Company.

The natural world of Carmel is showcased in these photographs by local photographer Richard A. Bucich. Clockwise from upper left: brilliant ice plants at Pacific Grove; monarch butterflies; gray whale flukes; and the ever-popular sea otter. Courtesy of the photographer.

XI
Environment and Wildlife

Robinson Jeffers was the first to write about preserving the Carmel area's natural beauty. The entire central coast is rich with plant, animal and marine life.

More than 100 species of birds, over 300 various species of fish, and 30 types of marine mammals live in the Carmel coastal areas. On any given day, it's possible to watch pods of dolphins or grey whales, sea lions, sea otters, herons, pelicans, and of course the ubiquitous sea gulls. No wonder the Ohlone Indians and the Chinese immigrants stayed at the shore where food was so abundant.

MONTEREY BAY SANCTUARY

Monterey Bay is home to the largest marine canyon in the United States. The canyon lies two miles below the ocean's surface, and is estimated to be ten million years old. In 1992, Monterey Bay officially became a National Marine Sanctuary, the country's largest, and with very good reason. Because of sanctuary designation, there is now a permanent ban on oil drilling in Carmel and Monterey Bays, the Pebble Beach coastline and Big Sur.

Years of negotiations and political maneuvering preceded the designation. United States Congressman Leon Panetta, Governor Pete Wilson, United States Senator Alan Cranston, President George Bush, Energy Secretary James Watkins and Interior Secretary Donald Hodel were involved in the movement toward sanctuary status. In 1985, a preliminary agreement had prevented drilling until the year 2000. When Hodel backed down on that agreement, Panetta introduced legislation in 1986 that demanded Monterey Bay Sanctuary become a reality. His bill passed in 1988 but before it could take effect in 1989, President George Bush reneged and approved oil development.

Persistent California residents gathered scientific information from the National Oceanic and Atmospheric Administration that proved that the California coastal areas should be saved from oil drilling. In the end, President Bush agreed and the bay obtained its designation.

Today, the 400-mile coastal area which begins immediately north of San Francisco and extends as far south as San Simeon is protected from oil exploration, airplane flights lower than 100 feet, and jet skiing. There is no restriction on ship traffic, however.

The Sanctuary will eventually incorporate a 35-mile trail system that will connect with Elkhorn Slough. Portions of the trail are completed but ad-

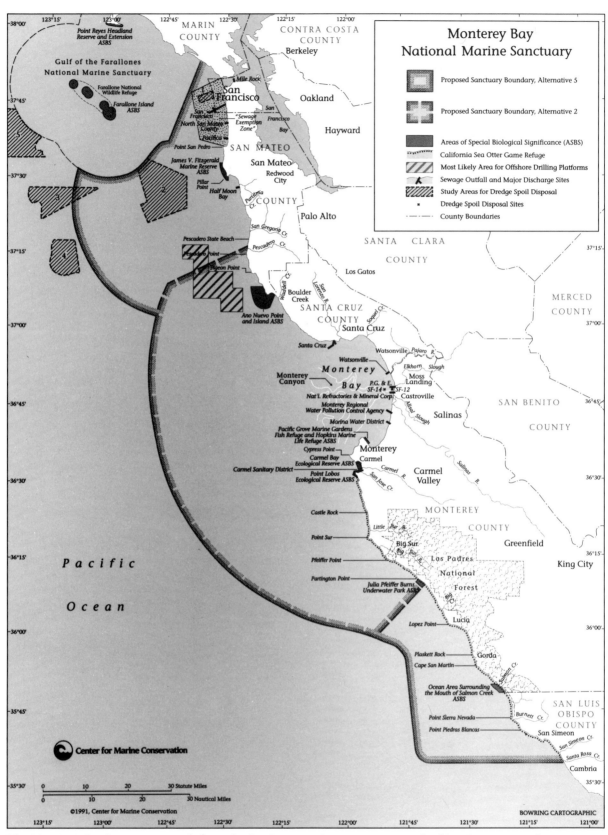

Monterey Bay National Marine Sanctuary

- Proposed Sanctuary Boundary, Alternative 5
- Proposed Sanctuary Boundary, Alternative 2
- Areas of Special Biological Significance (ASBS)
- California Sea Otter Game Refuge
- Most Likely Area for Offshore Drilling Platforms
- Sewage Outfall and Major Discharge Sites
- Study Areas for Dredge Spoil Disposal
- Dredge Spoil Disposal Sites
- County Boundaries

The Monterey Bay Sanctuary extends from the San Francisco Bay area to just south of San Simeon. Map by Bowring Cartographic, and the Center for Marine Conservation.

106

ditional work is continuing to connect all coastal areas in the trail system. Other protected areas include designated wetlands on the Mission Ranch, two smaller wetlands in the Spanish Bay golf course in Pebble Beach, and wetlands at the mouth of the Salinas River, Crespi Pond in the Pacific Grove golf course, and at Point Pinos.

ELKHORN SLOUGH AND WETLANDS

Elkhorn Slough is California's largest coastal wetland, and it lies in the northern part of Monterey County near Moss Landing. This seven-mile-long river channel of 2500 acres may be just a swamp to most people, but it is an important sanctuary. Various species of fish seek out the slough to lay eggs and return to the ocean.

More than 100 species of local and migratory birds make the area a birdwatchers haven, with some birds migrating from as far away as the Arctic. Elkhorn Slough is open to the public for hiking and canoeing.

Only through the efforts of several organizations and individuals was this area saved. California's State Fish and Game Department, the State Department of Parks and Recreation, and philanthropist David Packard are some of the entities that made the slough a possibility. It is significant to California because most of the wetlands in the state have been destroyed.

CONSERVATION AREAS

Both Pebble Beach and Carmel have gardens where native plant life is showcased. The Samuel F. B. Morse Botanical Gardens was in the path of the devastating Pebble Beach fire in 1988 which destroyed homes, and plant and animal life. Morse's

early plans kept Pebble Beach from being totally developed and have provided riding and hiking trails and open space forest and coastal areas.

Carmel maintains open space at Devendorf Park in the town's limits, the Mission Trail near the Mission Ranch, and the Flanders Mansion, the site of the Lester Rowntree Arboretum.

Gertrude Ellen Lester Rowntree was an author of plant books and married to a former Carmel City Council member, Bernard Rowntree. He was a dedicated preservationist who helped save several Monterey adobes. She traveled throughout the west collecting seeds and plantings. A citizens group, which formed in 1980, cares for the arboretum. Paul Flanders built the large home directly to the west of the arboretum in 1924. In the 1980s the city purchased the property which now forms a 40-acre park.

Carmel tried to be ahead of the environmental era when residents agreed to a recycling program in 1989 that includes the use of colored baskets for sorting items. Ironically, however, in 1992 Carmel requested that the state slow the recycling law because of costs. Residents and businesses will have to pay fees totalling more than $6 million over a 15-year period in order to have their recyclable items picked up and processed.

The Lone Cypress Tree, heralded as a symbol for Pebble Beach, is several hundred years old. The weather-worn tree is located above the Pacific Ocean on rock outcroppings near Cypress Point and is a main tourist attraction on the 17 Mile Drive. Vandals tried to destroy the tree a few years ago but it was saved. Now it is held in place by cables and continues to be a symbol of strength that has endured for centuries.

Approximately 48 percent of the land in Pebble Beach is open space, or about 2500 of its 5200 acres including golf courses. There are forest reserves in Pebble Beach which include the Crocker Grove of Cypress Trees on the 17 Mile Drive.

The Del Monte Land Use Plan in Pebble Beach was certified by the California Coastal Commission and includes areas of open space like the Pescadero Canyon corridor, which borders between Carmel and Pebble Beach, the upper Pebble Beach Huckleberry Hill area which burned in 1989, the 83-acre Morse Reserve and Indian Village. The Spanish Bay Dunes are also protected. There are specific restrictions in the plan for the number of dwellings still allowed to be built, the type of residences, and the acreage to be maintained for shops or additional reserves.

BUTTERFLIES

Pacific Grove, which calls itself "Butterfly Town, U.S.A.," is the migratory destination of the monarch butterfly. Those that arrive one year are really three generations from the butterflies who came the previous year. The monarchs arrive through December and stay through March. During this period, the Friends of the Monarchs, an organization that helps protect the butterflies, display signs that alert motorists to "brake for butterflies" and one that states "Caution: Butterfly Zone." Friends of the Monarch is also spearheading a movement to make the butterfly our national insect.

The current monarch sanctuary, a nearly three-acre site within the town, contains Monterey pine and eucalyptus trees. These butterfly trees hold massive clusters of the monarchs. The original habitat in George Washington Park, on Pine and Alder Streets, was filled with ancient trees that no longer provide adequate habitat for the monarchs.

The 1991 Pacific Grove City Council approved the establishment of the Monarch Habitat Restoration Committee. The monarch sanctuary land is being purchased by a local tax assessment, and the Washington Park area is being reseeded through community effort.

Recent harsh winters in Mexico froze the monarch groves, killing off about 90% of the eastern migration. Logging in Mexico has also reduced timber habitats. Heat and drought in California has greatly reduced the monarch population in recent years.

BIG SUR PRESERVATION

In 1972, Proposition 20 established the California Coastal Zone Commission, and a plan for the preservation and development of the Big Sur coastline. This plan included private stewardship of the land, rather than government involvement, a point highly regarded by the descendants of pioneer families.

An opposing group led by Ansel Adams, architect Will Shaw, Larry Moss, State Representative Sam Farr and William Turnage wanted Big Sur preserved by making it into a national park and placed under federal control. The Nature Conservancy, which acquires land for future preservation as does the Big Sur Land Trust, occasionally transfers land. Adams was vice president of the Big Sur Land Trust. Several groups formed to find solutions to the debate over Big Sur's future.

Architect Nathaniel Owings and his wife, Margaret Wentworth Owings, proposed a mixture of private, state and national control for the preservation and development of Big Sur land holdings. In 1976, the Coastal Conservation Act demanded the establishment of a master plan for development of the area. A task force was chaired by Gary Koeppel, owner of the Coast Gallery. It was Koeppel who also chaired the Big Sur Citizens Committee which sought to forestall any move on the part of environmentalists until all the issues were discussed. Another group, the Central Coast Commission, battled residents over restrictions such as scenic easements on Alan Funt's large ranch and sculptor Emil Norman's property. The general feeling was that big government should stay out of Big Sur.

In 1981, legislation was enacted that gave owners a Transfer of Development Credit for a critical view shed designated on the master plan. The credit can be traded for land located inland so that the coastline will not be hidden by development. A minimum parcel size of forty acres for any development or building was established, and mining and logging restrictions were also imposed.

The Save the Redwoods organization and the Packard Foundation donated land holdings for preservation through the Nature Conservancy so these properties would remain undeveloped.

A group called Friends of the Big Sur Coast consisted of long-time residents and descendants of pioneer families in Big Sur, and was chaired by James Moser Josoff. The group traveled to Washington, D.C. in 1980 and again in 1986 to oppose federal legislation and lobby senators who were to decide if Big Sur would become a national scenic area.

They met with then Senators Pete Wilson and Alan Cranston and others to appeal the decision proposed by those two legislators. One of the residents' main arguments was that even without the area having national designation, three million people annually visit Big Sur anyway. This delegation of residents and others felt strongly that the residents could better preserve the area than the government. They also contended that the national park system did not have funds to properly maintain its current holdings. Adding Big Sur would be another expense to the government and probably prove detrimental in the long run to the area.

The question was: would these residents have to continually appeal to the senators in Washington, D.C. in order to preserve their private property rights? There was also opposition to making Highway One a toll road through Big Sur. Frank Trotter's appeal as the son of pioneer Trotters brought everyone to the height of emotion.

Big Sur's vast acreage in state and national holdings includes the Pfeiffer-Big Sur and Julia Pfeiffer Burns State Parks, the Ventana Wilderness, Garrapata Beach State Park, the Point Sur Lighthouse State Historical Park, and the 196,400-acre Los Padres National Forest. (Los Padres was first declared by President Theodore Roosevelt in 1903; in 1936 it was given its present name by President Franklin D. Roosevelt in honor of the Franciscan fathers for their founding of the eight missions located near the forest.) Ventana Wilderness has been a sanctuary for the California condor.

Myles Williams, former member of the Christy Minstrels, co-owns the Post Ranch Inn, a Big Sur hotel that takes pains to minimize its impact on the environment. Courtesy of the photographer, Kathleen Olson.

Because of controls on development in Big Sur, it may seem surprising that a hotel was built there in 1992 across from the Ventana Inn. The Post Ranch Inn has taken every precaution to coordinate with the environment. Only one tree was cut for the 30-room inn, and that was because the county felt it was a fire hazard. The owners, Myles Williams (a member of the Christy Minstrels singing group during the 1960s) and his partner,

attorney Michael Freed, purchased the land which was once part of the Willard Post Ranch.

TREES

Trees in the Carmel area are nearly sacred to residents. Friends of the Carmel Forest was formed in 1992 and set about contacting all the Carmel households, suggesting that residents plant a native pine tree. Trees there are valued by an official national arboral mathematical configuration.

Trees of historic significance are identified in Carmel. Until twenty years ago, trees were numbered but today they are inventoried only. The town's largest tree is a Eucalyptus nearly twenty-three feet around.

In the 1930s a Carmel tree commission was given the authority to decide which trees should be cut down. Carmel Mayor P. A. McGreery, who served from 1942–1946, recommended that those important decisions be made by the entire city council rather than a separate commission.

In 1990, a Fresno, California contractor, Patrick Shepherd, damaged a 100-year-old Monterey Pine. The tree was 50 percent severed and its root system was no longer able to support the tree, so the city fined the contractor an astounding $24,000.

More recently, a pine tree was encroaching on Peter Levy's house in Carmel. When it came to deciding whether the tree or the house would go, the Carmel City Council, on appeal, voted to remove the tree. However, Levy was required to gather the tree's seeds so it could live on.

Carmel's trees are protected by city ordinance. This cypress on Camino Real measures over fifteen feet around its trunk. Courtesy of Isabelle Hall and the *Carmel Sun*.

WILDLIFE

One of the area's most exciting moments on the central coast was the rediscovery of the sea otters. Sea otters are entertaining to watch. They will actually find a rock, hold it until they find shellfish like crabs or seastars, go to the surface, hold the rock on their chests and pound the shellfish until it opens. They've been known to do the same thing with aluminum cans in search of octopuses. They groom themselves after dinner, too.

In 1913 California passed laws protecting the sea otters with a $1000 penalty; it is also a federal offense for possessing or taking sea otters. But even so, through the 1930s the otter population started dwindling.

Those little critters are blamed for depleting the abalone population, however. Years ago, sea otters were killed for their pelts, and when the otter population was depleted accordingly, the abalone became numerous.

In 1985 sea otters were further protected with the introduction of a bill that banned inshore gill-net fishing from the entire central coast because otters would sometimes get caught in the nets. Today the otter population is thriving along the coast once again. Friends of the Sea Otter is an active organization with 5000 members that takes all measures to protect the otters and educate the public.

Sea otters—which are related to minks, weasels, skunks and badgers—can always be observed in their natural habitats along the Carmel, Pebble Beach and Monterey coastline. Sitting in a Fisherman's Wharf restaurant in Monterey, it is common to watch the sea otters cracking abalone shells on their chests with gulls and pelicans nearby.

Brown pelicans dive into the water off Carmel Bay, often enough for observers to see them as they walk along Carmel Beach. Cormorants, grebes, ducks, and seagulls are everywhere. Hawks, owls, blackbirds, turkey vultures, sparrows, finches and the popular quail are easily observed on the central coast. Scrub jays are found in scrub oak and chapar-

Scenic Drive in Carmel was once a long archway of trees. Courtesy of the Local History Department, Harrison Memorial Library.

ral in Big Sur. Stellar jays are found in coastal forests and the nearby mountains.

In Big Sur, wild pigs, coyotes, cougars, and black bears live in the forests and mountains. Elephant seals and dolphin can often be observed offshore.

Pebble Beach has its share of raccoons, deer and quail. Herds of deer at various times of the day are seen on the golf courses and interrupt play. Bird and Seal Rocks in Pebble Beach are filled with sea lions lolling in their natural habitat. Sea otters are seen in special places, too, along the 17-Mile Drive in kelp beds where they play and rest.

Grey whales migrate 10,000 miles annually from the Bering Sea to Baja California. Nearly 20,000 whales pass the area and some even enter Monterey Bay during their migrations. Their dotted backs and fins are seen from shore especially during their migration season, from December through February, and later in the year when they return northward. Sometimes the whales are going in two different directions at once, some north and some south. The grey whales have been dropped from the endangered species list because of protective measures taken years ago to save them.

The best places to watch for these giant creatures are at Cypress Point in Pebble Beach, Point Lobos State Reserve, Garrapata Beach in Big Sur, and at Point Pinos in Pacific Grove.

Tidal pools are found in smooth worn sandstone bases along the coast where the tide waters are captured, especially in December and June when the tide is led away by the sun and moon. Anemones with tentacles that float, sea urchins with spikes, star fish and snails make their home in tidal pools.

The entire Carmel area is a vast natural wonder—a spectacular meeting of land, sea, and people. Despite its occasionally contentious politics and conflicting views over land use, Carmel's rich history and unique setting are revered by all who live there.

XII
Not Politics As Usual

Politics played a significant role in Carmel-by-the-Sea long before Clint Eastwood became mayor. Visitors to Carmel observe a gorgeous seashore and lovely quaint cottages, but beyond the facade of a fairy tale village is a real city with many of the problems of a much larger one.

Whether feuding about parking, trees, commercial zoning, ice cream cones, or the need for a dam and additional sources of water, Carmel residents are often embroiled in conflicts, pettiness, and political battles. It's politics that keep Carmel alive.

Nearly 5,000 residents live in Carmel-By-The-Sea, with an average age of over 55. Many residents live on fixed incomes and could not repurchase their own homes. Since 1990, however, high-income management types from larger California cities have been purchasing the expensive properties, renovating and rebuilding the older ones.

Perry Newberry wasn't the only person to campaign to stop Carmel from growing and changing. Some of the more outspoken mayors such as Fred Godwin, Gunnar Norberg, and Charlotte Townsend tried to maintain the town's character at the cost of resident's rights. Liberal attitudes have been met with resistance.

THE RADICALS

Starting in the 1940s with Big Sur resident and author Henry Miller's liberal views, Carmel has taken action against those perceived as left-leaning. At that time, Mayor Fred Godwin, a critic of Miller's politics, said Carmel had no room for radicals. He quickly complimented the American Legion when it had dispersed crowds of these young people by using force, namely clubs, in Carmel.

There were more peaceful ways of working through these problems. One Carmel resident visited his Big Sur cabin to find uninvited transients in a vacant nearby shack. He threw fish into his fireplace and the odor sent the people running in the opposite direction with the man shouting that he would cook a skunk the next time.

In the 1960s, when another liberal group descended on the town, more action was taken again, and successfully.

One of Carmel's most highly regarded former mayors is Barney Laiolo, who served three terms as mayor: 1968–1970, 1970–1972 and 1980–1982. He also served on Carmel's Planning Commission. After moving to Carmel in 1945, Laiolo started his Village Radio Electric business on Mission Street. Later he joined the Lois Renk Realty business. In

Carmel's three-term mayor Barney Laiolo and his wife, Elinor, celebrate her election as council member in 1986. Courtesy of the *Carmel Pine Cone.*

1948 he served on Carmel's one and only jury trial of a Carmel man who refused to pay a fine after hitting a fence with his car.

He left real estate when he ran for mayor in 1968. That year, Carmel appeared to be threatened by a large group of what some people called "undesirables." They were hippies, quite simply, and they loitered in the town's Devendorf Park and challenged people to walk over them rather than move.

Laiolo dressed rather creatively in various disguises each day and patrolled the park with a camera, a police radio, and a gun. He observed drug

deals, took photographs of the offenders, and radioed the police who made quick arrests. To further control the area, he patrolled the beach on foot. When the Kiwanis Club donated a dune buggy, his patrols were cut to 20 minutes per evening.

Laiolo established a clever regulation that peacefully dispersed the hippies. The City Council simply approved watering the park every 15 minutes! Ann Parr, the wife of a local radio talk show host, challenged the rule saying it was unfair and that the hippies had rights, too. (Robert Fischer, a policeman who arrested Parr for obstructing the law, was later elevated to the Carmel City Council.) The case went to court but was later dismissed. By that time, the hippies had moved away. The town considered Laiolo a hero of sorts for taking action, but he made other contributions, too. Laiolo was the first mayor to write a weekly mayor's report in the *Carmel Pine Cone,* and he successfully negotiated with William Doolittle for 17 acres of land at the Mission Trail Park, southeast of the town's limits, as open space.

In 1971, Gunnar Norberg wanted to create a "Heritage City." His proposal included the stipulation that if property with commercial zoning was unused for a period of three years, it would be changed back to residential. It also included the same powers of the state to take over fire, school, and sanitation districts. The California State Legislature Assembly Committee on Local Government decided the Legislature would not authorize a city to have the same powers as a state. Norberg's idea was dropped but surfaced again in the 1980s.

Politics became heated again after Laiolo lost his

bid for a fourth mayoral term in 1982 to Charlotte Townsend. Her anti-growth doctrine was supported by the previous anti-growth mayor, Gunnar Norberg, and his followers. Townsend's administration worked on a general plan for the city that included some controversial private-property restrictions.

As businesses closed or their leases expired, they were replaced with more resident-serving businesses. This was in keeping with the priorities set in the 1929 Magna Carta. The town seemed innundated with restrictions and an attitude of apathy prevailed under Townsend's administration. By 1985 there was little citizen input at meetings because many residents speculated that decisions were being made in closed door sessions.

ICE CREAM

It was during this time that the town's ice cream cone issue became a national scandal. After all, what kind of town didn't allow ice cream parlors or permit people to buy ice cream cones and walk down the streets with them?

The issue came about when the lease on Swenson's Ice Cream Parlor on Ocean Avenue was to expire on September 1, 1985. Carmel resident Mary Lawson had operated that national franchise for fifteen years. William Lawson, her son and successor, knew in January 1985 that the lease would not be renewed. After searching for several months, Lawson applied for a new location at the Wishart Bakery on Ocean Avenue but was turned down by the Carmel City Council. The council did not want an ice cream shop on Ocean Avenue.

This early Carmel shop featured Mr. Curtis's homemade candy and ice cream. In 1985 the town became known as "scrooge city" after banning ice cream shops. Courtesy of the Local History Department, Harrison Memorial Library.

Lawson then found the Carmel Barber Shop location owned by Harold Wamsley.

While Lawson was applying for a new permit in August 1985, the council passed a water ordinance which made it unlawful to relocate a water use permit even for the same kind of business. So the town was without an ice cream shop. This gave rise to Carmel's famous ice cream cone flap, Carmel's moratorium of sorts on ice cream shops, and the town being called "Scrooge City." Clint Eastwood called it "un-American" that a town wouldn't allow ice cream parlors.

Lawson was told he would have to wait months before the planning commission could hear the matter, even though he chose not to continue the franchise operation but wanted an independent one at the bakery site. At the same time, Michael Montana and his partner James Newhouse applied for a business permit for an ice cream parlor called Carmel Creamery on Mission Street. Their permit was also denied because of the ordinance on water use permits.

By this time the 1986 mayoral campaign was in full swing and any new decisions on the applications would not be made until after the election of council members and a new mayor. After the election, when it appeared that Montana was going to receive a permit for an ice cream parlor at the Wishart Bakery location, Lawson took legal action.

He filed a lawsuit on September 15, 1986 in Monterey County Superior Court against the City of Carmel-by-the-Sea claiming he was not given equal treatment, his civil rights had been violated, and that the city intentionally interfered with business relations.

Later in 1986, Michael Lajigian was allowed to open a store selling gellatto, but only after the city council approved the definition of gellatto being a "frozen dessert"—not ice cream!

Lawson thereupon abandoned the notion of owning an ice cream business in Carmel.

RUN CLINT RUN

Why would a world-famous actor, director, and producer run for mayor of a small town of 5,000 residents? How did it happen?

By 1985, residents were becoming more disenchanted with Townsend's second term as mayor. Among those residents was Clint Eastwood. Many things happened at once.

While Carmel was being called "Scrooge City" for not selling ice cream cones, Eastwood was trying to obtain a commercial building permit, and private meetings of several of Carmel's long-time prominent residents were taking place. Glenn Leidig, Barney Laiolo, Robert Evans, Clyde Sturges, and Clint Eastwood were some of the people attending those meetings to discuss their displeasure with the Townsend regime.

Eastwood had applied for a permit for a commercial building adjacent to the Hog's Breath, a restaurant he co-owned with Walter Becker. Carmel-by-the-Sea merchants tell the same story of tourists who pop in their establishments only to ask, "Where's the Hog's Breath?"

Like anyone else, Eastwood went through the complete permit process. His permit was turned down several times by the planning commission. After an April 1985 denial, Eastwood appealed to the Carmel City Council. His building plans included an elevator shaft which exceeded Carmel's height limit and he needed a variance. Sitting on the council was a postal employee named David Maradei, an outspoken opponent of Eastwood's project. If Eastwood, the director, was casting the role of villain, he may have given it to Maradei.

Jim Miller

Carmel · by · the · Sea

Patiently, like a big cat waiting for its prey, Eastwood took the route of least resistance and waited through the appeal process, having his architect make the specified changes. He even personally appeared at council meetings quietly sitting in the back of the room. Eastwood's permit was denied by the council, which said in a letter that his building was too big, had too much glass and was not in keeping with the town's character.

Eastwood filed a lawsuit against the City of Carmel-by-the-Sea which was entered in Monterey County Superior Court. There was a principle behind it: if the actor was treated this way, one could only imagine what was happening to less famous residents. The lawsuit forced the council's hand and design changes were negotiated with Eastwood. His permit was finally approved later in 1985.

In October 1985, Eastwood surprised members of the Carmel Business Association by attending their breakfast meeting at the La Playa Hotel. In quite certain terms, he made it known that he wasn't at all pleased with the Townsend administration nor its negativity toward residents and the way they were treated.

At private meetings taking place during the same period, everyone agreed that, in the town's best interest and that of the citizens, a change in the administration was absolutely necessary. The group asked Barney Laiolo to run for mayor against Townsend again.

After consideration, Laiolo said he was not afraid to run against her again, but this time the race needed someone who could win handily. Those at the private meetings immediately looked to Eastwood as the best candidate. Many people thought it was all a "set up" to corner the actor into running for mayor.

The carrot was offered and Eastwood nibbled, but he wasn't going to run in the race without knowing if he could win it. Perhaps it was to him like knowing if a film would sell before spending millions of dollars to make it.

Eastwood hired a Southern California firm to poll the residents and the results were quite surprising. The poll showed that Townsend's administration was negatively perceived by the residents. Although more name recognition went to Elinor Laiolo, the wife of the former mayor, Eastwood came in a strong second; good enough to give it a try, perhaps, but he kept his hat on a little longer to think about it.

When he decided to submit his candidate's papers shortly before the deadline on January 30, 1986, and throw his hat into the political arena, city council bids from Elinor Laiolo and former Carmel policeman, Robert Fischer, came along with them. Although the three were never a "ticket," they did ally themselves on most of the issues throughout the campaign.

Speculation ran high that Eastwood was running only because he was angry with the planning commission's and the council's treatment of his permit. Shouts of vengeance came from the opposition on many occasions. But the die was cast. From that day forward, for two years, the town was never the same.

Candidates Clint Eastwood, incumbent Charlotte Townsend, and Paul Laub smile at a forum during the 1986 campaign. Courtesy of the *Monterey Bay Tribune*.

THE CAMPAIGN THAT LIT THE TOWN

Academy Award-winning director and producer Clint Eastwood didn't ride into town one day on a big, white horse smoking a cigar, although it seemed that way to many people. Eastwood first visited the area in the 1940s with his family as tourists. He later became familiar with the area during his army days at Fort Ord on the Monterey Peninsula, where he taught swimming.

The star, a very private and quiet man, moved to the peninsula and has lived there for more than twenty years, first in Pebble Beach with his former wife, Maggie Eastwood Wynberg, and their two children, Kyle and Alison, and now in Carmel.

Clint Eastwood the candidate made his political debut on Friday, February 21, 1986, at the Carmel Republican Women's Club forum. An over-capacity crowd of nearly 300 residents filled the Crossroads Community Room that evening, anxious to see the candidate and the man. There were four mayoral candidates in the race, but only the three registered Republican candidates were invited to speak that night.

The public listened to the diversity of timed presentations by the 55-year-old millionaire movie actor, Paul Laub, a 41-year-old businessman and owner of several tourist–oriented shops, and the 61-year-old woman incumbent, Charlotte Townsend. Timothy Grady, the environmentalist candidate, singer, and youngest of the four, was not invited to participate.

Eastwood appeared a bit nervous and quite serious; Townsend looked stern; and Laub smiled as he would throughout the campaign. Using my media and public relations background, I not only coordinated the entire forum, but the question and answer session and news conference, too. With a cordless microphone, à la the Donahue Show, I went into the audience to seek questions for the candidates. One woman stared at Eastwood and promptly forgot her question; another told the actor how great looking he was in person; and a third simply asked if he remembered her.

Throughout that evening and the ensuing campaign, the same question was asked of Eastwood: "Are you serious?" The answer was always "Yes." Eastwood told everyone Carmel was his home and he cared about it.

Eastwood's platform included criticism of the town's lack of financial support for the Carmel Youth Center, which later became one of his personal projects as mayor. He opposed the town's litigation against its neighbor, Pebble Beach, over closing the Carmel gate and the potential development of the Inn at Spanish Bay. He fiercely supported private property rights.

Eastwood spoke strongly against what he called the "Gestapo" tactics of the Townsend administration, which wanted to pass a general plan that would forbid second kitchens or studio apartments in Carmel homes. The division between commercial and resident interests was often debated. He wanted to bring back the days of camaraderie in Carmel. He favored the library expansion and the immediate building of a parking facility at the Sunset Center.

All the mayoral candidates agreed that the city should purchase the Mission Ranch property which

The Pebble Beach gate into Carmel became a point of contention among the candidates in the 1986 mayoral race. Courtesy of the Pat Hathaway Collection.

was located outside the town's limits to save it from development. Residents often discussed this issue with Eastwood which became a harbinger to his later purchase of the property.

At the forum, with a microphone in hand, I had the distinct experience of saying, "Excuse me, Mr. Eastwood, but your time is up." He gave me a serious look straight from one of his movies, complete with the famous squint. When I smiled, however, (what else could I do?) he whispered "thank you" and sat down like the other candidates.

That evening a news conference followed the forum to allow the local media a chance to meet the candidates. Even though I gave the paid security guards a specific list and instructions to follow, a woman identifying herself as a reporter from the *National Enquirer* got into the conference. This upset Eastwood, but he realized there were limitations. It would be next to impossible to keep the national media out of the campaign.

On February 25, the Monterey Bay Republican Women's Club sponsored their forum at the Holiday Inn on Rio Road, now known as the Carmel Mission Inn, and Eastwood seemed much more relaxed. Afterward, however, the star candidate was besieged by reporters, TV cameras, and more than 200 luncheon guests. Two women came to his rescue that day. While Ramona Smith, the president of the Carmel Republican Women's Club, made her way to Eastwood, I drove my car to the front of the hotel.

As both Smith and Eastwood entered the car, the TV cameramen filmed the license plates and placed their cameras up to my window. The media wanted to know about everything and everyone involved in the star's campaign. The amusing part of the "rescue" was that the three of us simply drove around to the back of the hotel where Eastwood's car was parked.

The biggest challenges to his campaign were keeping the media in control and convincing residents that he was sincere. He was one of the rare candidates who didn't need publicity or name recognition. He had that on a daily basis.

Although he didn't want the election to become a media circus, it seemed like every known media representative from around the world arrived in Carmel. Eastwood, with the long and graceful strides of a gazelle, became a master at maneuvering Carmel's alleyways that skirt through the business district.

The day of the second forum, Eastwood met for the first time with Sue Hutchinson, the paid, political campaign manager he hired from Southern California. She took control of his political life throughout the campaign and later during his term as mayor. Eastwood, the man in control of his own multi-million dollar productions, gave up control of this portion of his life to this experienced campaign fundraiser from Huntington Beach, who had previously worked on the offshore oil drilling issue in Santa Barbara. She knew more about campaigns than he did, but his managerial style often called for using experts in their own fields.

Many times throughout the campaign, Hutchinson was referred to as Eastwood's right-hand man. Her occasional abrasive manner turned off the locals when she heavily screened them out. But Eastwood was paying her to do a job, and she was doing it.

However, bringing in a professional campaign manager, one who wasn't familiar with Carmel, had many residents, especially the opposition, shouting "big politics." Suddenly, what could be a home-town campaign began looking like a polished plot in one of Eastwood's movies.

During our first conversation about the campaign, I had offered to help Eastwood with the media because I had already established a rapport with the locals and knew people across the country. When Eastwood invited me to meet with him and his campaign manager, I told both of them that Clint did not need any publicity. What he needed was to get his own message across and say only what he wanted repeated. Eastwood liked what I said. I offered him a resume and he said he didn't need it. "I can tell about people," he said to me.

He asked me to work directly with him, inde-

Gary Trudeau's Doonesbury comic strip took accurate aim at Carmel's 1986 mayoral campaign, and brought the town more of what it didn't want—national publicity. Doonesbury copyright 1986 G. B. Trudeau. Reprinted with permission of Universal Press Syndicate. All rights reserved.

pendent of the campaign and his campaign manager, to coordinate the media activities, including two televised debates. Throughout the campaign and during his term of office, I worked completely behind the scenes because he said I would have more power and be able to pull more strings that way. It was true. Members of the media, from locals to network producers, knew what I was doing, but Carmel residents had no idea.

I kept my word to the media and did not have any problems. In fact, on one occasion, I asked a nationally known photographer not to take photos at one event. I promised him an opportunity to personally meet with Eastwood if he cooperated. All it took was communication and I wasn't intimidated by the media. Clint said I wasn't intimidated by *him,* either! He said I must be use to working with people like him. Well, that was a bit of a stretch. There really isn't anyone like him at all.

More than 100 volunteers appeared at Eastwood's first rally at his campaign headquarters, located next to his restaurant in what was an old art gallery building. The gallery and a tree nursery were located on the property that would later become Eastwood's commercial building and the source of his original problems with the city council. Eastwood's most active volunteers were a mix of older Carmel residents, including his neighbor Marguerite MacLaughlin, Phyllis Howard, hotel owner Clyde Sturges, businessman Jack Gibson, restauranteur Bud Allen, and the owner of Fortier's Drugstore, Florence Berrey. A volunteer, David Archer, served as a bodyguard, ran errands for Hutchinson, and as we shall see later, shocked the entire community.

Eastwood's two close personal friends, Phil Dacey, who was in the advertising business, and Jim Freeman, a teacher who gathered the youth votes, were nearly always at his side.

Buttons and brochures were produced by the volunteers with little, if any, of Eastwood's direction or approval. Two Eastwood buttons, one with a dated photograph of the star in a ruffled shirt, became collector's items. That was the flashiest part of the entire campaign. Most of the time,

Eastwood dressed casually and didn't even wear his watch. He made every effort to keep the campaign low-key and as much a grass-roots campaign as was humanly possible given the constraints of his fame. Others, like candidate Paul Laub, were capitalizing on Eastwood's name by selling souvenir T-shirts. At one point I suggested that Clint stop those sales, but he said it would sound like "sour grapes." After the election, however, Clint did object to such sales unless the funds were directed to the Carmel Youth Foundation.

Eastwood made himself available to the residents, and in the process attended about 52 neighborhood teas where voters could meet him. The actor, who became famous for his one-liners in Italian westerns and some rather violent movies, used his persuasive powers to convince voters he was serious about the campaign and the town.

His support grew in numbers and eventually included people from the opposition. Gunnar Norberg was convinced that Eastwood would maintain the town's character, and he still hoped his Heritage City idea might become a reality with Eastwood at the helm. Others like Harriette Rowntree, and Marjory Lloyd who was once the editor of the *Carmel Pine Cone* and an active member of Carmel's historical group, Carmel Heritage, supported him also. Jean Grace openly admitted that she was unsure about him in the beginning of his campaign, but that Eastwood had won her vote, too. It was Grace who succeeded Eastwood as mayor in 1988.

Eastwood's unlisted phone number became a point of contention. Residents wondered how available he would be if elected. The environmentalist candidate, Timothy Grady, wasn't concerned about late-night calls. He didn't have a phone at all.

Eastwood had to convince the voters that he wouldn't be an absentee mayor. Being a man of his word, he refused to make hollow campaign promises as most politicians do for votes. He never promised he wouldn't leave town, nor did he promise to stop making movies. When Townsend's campaign charged that Eastwood was a developer, he never denied it.

Townsend stood at the post office handing out her brochures, Laub went door–to–door, and Eastwood attended teas. There was nothing normal about this campaign. How could there be when a world-famous actor runs for a two-year mayoral term at $200 per month in a one-square-mile town with 5,000 residents? *Normal* didn't describe the more than 100 members of the national media descending on the town, or the interview requests from Japan, Italy, France, and England that frequently came.

The lengthiest of the forums was held at the All Saints Episcopal Church on March 18. Townsend's attack on Eastwood as a "disgruntled developer" brought boos. When Eastwood addressed the second-kitchen issues, he received thunderous applause. The crowd broke into laughter when Grady said he lived at one time on the dunes at Spanish Bay.

More residents than ever registered to vote during the campaign. As a contrast to the 1984 city council elections, when only about 900 voters registered out of 4000, the 1986 election saw about 4,000 registered voters out of nearly 5,000 residents.

The League of Women Voters investigated rumors of voter registration fraud that included the names of some of Eastwood's supporters such as Richard Lugo and Clyde Sturges. The league was led to believe that some of Eastwood's supporters, business owners in particular, were not residents of Carmel-by-the-Sea, but used their business addresses in Carmel as voting resident addresses. After those charges were made by League president Lorita Fisher, Townsend called what she thought was going to be a private press conference on the steps of Town Hall on the evening of April 1. Eastwood, however, surprised the incumbent by appearing with supporters to answer accusations.

Some strong statements were made that evening, including one by Eastwood who told the opposition's campaign co-chairman, author Robert Irvine, to literally shut up. Eastwood charged that Maradei was responsible for the voter-fraud accusations but Maradei denied any wrongdoing. Eastwood came prepared that evening. He looked down his eyeglasses and quoted information about the California law that charges a misdemeanor if anyone intimidates a voter. The issue quieted down.

Eastwood was well coached by his campaign manager. Throughout the campaign and his term of office, Eastwood was briefed by Hutchinson on many issues, from the simplest to the most complicated. His interest, knowledge, and desire to make things happen caught most residents by surprise. He was proving to be a very credible candidate.

Carmel was in the midst of litigation against the Pebble Beach Company and the Odello family, which owned a large parcel of land to the south of the Carmel Mission that they wanted to develop. It appeared that Carmel solved its problems only by litigating. Eastwood strongly objected to this action. In fact, if elected he offered to meet with his friend, Tom Oliver, the president of the Pebble Beach Company, and discuss the issues.

Eastwood continued being the soft-spoken, gracious candidate. On one occasion, he even assisted Townsend when the microphone at the La Playa Hotel presented problems during a debate.

"The Good, the Bad and the Ugly" became a sub-theme of the campaign, with everyone guessing who was who. Townsend was making charges left and right. From the way Eastwood's volunteers talked, outsiders might believe that Townsend was the Queen of Hearts, running around shouting "off with their heads!" The fact that her residence, located on the edge of Carmel-By-The-Sea's boundaries, was named "Town's End" was also grist for the mill. She had definite opinions about protecting the village character. Her campaign included a flyer with the drawing of a mother hen, representing the incumbent, watching over the town, while a hand with a dollar sign points a gun at the hen. What was left to protect? Practically every square inch was built on 40-foot lots.

In fact, she sounded like Perry Newberry by saying if the residents wanted more business involvement, traffic and tourists, they should vote for her opponents. She said Eastwood would make a better candidate in a big city where they need more tourists.

There were two local televised debates, two days apart. Hutchinson was openly nervous and apprehensive about Eastwood's appearance on TV during that first debate. Eastwood, dressed in a dark suit, appeared strained at the KSBW–TV debate on March 29. He occasionally gave the incumbent an unfriendly sideways glance. Two days later at the KMST-TV debate, he appeared more relaxed and even dressed in a lighter color.

The city council candidates, Laiolo and Fisher, were campaigning on their own. Laiolo, a former school administrator, spoke her mind and Fisher, the policeman, did the same. There would be diversity on the council, no matter who was elected.

A few days before the election, Paul Laub withdrew from the race knowing he couldn't carry the community's support. He asked everyone to vote for Eastwood. Laub had enjoyed basking in the star's limelight for a while.

Newspapers from *The Wall Street Journal* to the *Pomet* in Slobodna, Yugoslavia, carried front-page stories of Carmel's campaign. Eastwood was seen kissing babies on the campaign trail. More tourists came to Carmel, along with more media and more traffic. Everyone said it would go away when the election was over, but it didn't.

ELECTION DAY

On April 8, 1986, Carmel-by-the-Sea voters went to the polls. Eastwood dressed casually, voted at the All Saints Episcopal Church in the early morning, and took the day at an easy pace.

He spent about $30,000 on the campaign and Townsend spent only $2,000. The results were about as widespread and the margin of victory surprised even the star candidate.

A tabulation board was kept at Carmel's Sunset Center in Carpenter Hall, where about 130 members of the international media and 30 phone lines were ready for the results. The media waited patiently for the victors to appear for a news conference that evening. Microphones, cameras and lights were set up in anticipation as the evening drew to a close. Eastwood won by a two-thirds majority with 2166 votes. Townsend received 799, Grady 31, and Laub 6. Elinor Laiolo won her bid for city council with 1896 votes, and Fisher won with 1850. It was a landslide. Townsend conceded early that evening. The town had clearly mandated a change.

While the media waited at Carpenter Hall as their deadlines neared, a party was taking place in the La Playa Hotel's Poseidon Ballroom for Eastwood, Laiolo, and Fischer, where about 250 volunteers gathered to enjoy the moment of sweet victory. The victorious candidate kept the media at Carpenter Hall waiting for 45 minutes while he slipped away from the party and gave an interview at the Red Lion Restaurant, four blocks away.

There were no klieg lights, but nevertheless, Carmel was brightly lit. Bert Heron was the first actor to become involved in Carmel's politics but Eastwood would be the most famous to date.

When Eastwood, Laiolo, and Fisher arrived at the news conference, the media applauded. The new mayor was as gracious and soft spoken as always when he made a brief statement. When asked if he would run for president next, he definitively said, "No."

On Wednesday, the La Playa Hotel's gazebo garden was the site of a 1:00 p.m. news conference.

Mayor Clint Eastwood, a reporter, and fellow council members Robert Fischer, Robert Evans, and James Wright discuss the issues in Carmel. Courtesy of the *Carmel Pine Cone*.

Eastwood arrived holding a *Carmel Pine Cone* with his picture on the front page, and a small bag. Although the bag contained muffins from Katy's Cottage, he told the media "I brought my lunch." That, too, made the headlines.

President Ronald Reagan called to congratulate him that morning. They talked about how they both had worked with monkeys during their acting careers. James Stewart, whose movie *Mr. Smith Goes to Washington* was an influence on the new mayor, called, too.

It rained on April 15 when Eastwood and the new council members were inaugurated. The ceremonies were held outside City Hall under a large tent. While Eastwood was sworn in, his mother, Ruth Wood, watched proudly. Eastwood handed Townsend a miniature seedling pine, but there were no smiles exchanged. A large crowd stood in the rain, including his former wife, Maggie Eastwood Wynberg, who stopped with friends to watch the activities for a few minutes. When the ceremony was over, the Eastwood era began.

About a week later, the community was shocked to learn that one of Eastwood's volunteers had been arrested for murder. David Archer, who had been a visible part of the campaign, was later tried, convicted of murder, and sentenced to life in prison for the death of a Pebble Beach resident. During the trial, Archer tried to exploit his friendship with Eastwood and the campaign, but both the new mayor and Hutchinson denied any involvement or friendship with the man. Many doomsayer residents feared it would be a hint of things to come, but events would prove otherwise.

CALL ME CLINT

Eastwood dispensed with formalities and asked to be called by his first name, not Mayor Eastwood or Mr. Mayor. Just Clint.

The new mayor kept Hutchinson on the scene as his mayoral assistant. Eventually, even the *Carmel Pine Cone* and residents called Hutchinson the "stunt mayor" because she sat in on meetings, took his place on occasion, and basically took over city hall. She even shared the tiny mayor's office, although most often he was personally meeting with residents in town rather than spending time in city hall.

Many avoided city hall entirely and instead called Clint's production office in Burbank. I received calls from the media and residents, scripts, invitations, and every other odd request for Clint's participation. Unfortunately, many calls were unpleasant. Several residents wanted to serve on committees and were angered by the screening process. In reality, Clint did make himself available but it was, after all, only a part-time job he held as mayor. Considering the hours he spent on the issues, he made it more than a full-time job.

His council consisted of Laiolo, Fischer, longtime-resident Helen Arnold, and James Wright. His was only one vote out of five but he counted on the support of the two who were elected with him.

Six weeks after the gavel changed hands, the town was in an uproar because one of Clint's first acts as mayor was to fire six of the seven planning commission members. No sense in wasting time! Clint had given the commission weeks to perform differently than it had previously, and to serve the community in a better way. Ken White, who later became mayor in 1992, was allowed to remain on the commission.

Clint denied his action had anything to do with his personal experience with the commission, but he was accused of being vengeful once again. His action was seen as capricious for a number of reasons. Those commission members who were fired read about it in the *Carmel Pine Cone* before they were notified; furthermore, dismissing an entire commission required "emergency" designation. So, Clint took one step backward, declared an "emergency" because there was no commission, and the commission members were officially dismissed. Odd as it seems, that's Carmel politics.

The election was over but the opposition wasn't really giving up. Everything Clint's council did, every decision it made, was scrutinized. When the new mayor began his movie *Heartbreak Ridge* after being elected, the Townsend supporters were already claiming that he would be an absentee mayor

after all. But he wasn't—Eastwood never missed a regular city council meeting.

He began his term with the idea of running Carmel as a business. The meetings were meant to get right to the point. He promised to keep the meetings short and not waste time, but his first meeting as mayor included an agenda that contained so many issues it looked like a feature-length movie. It appeared Clint was going to solve all the town's problems at once. Public restrooms at the tiny Picadilly Park, the sale of Flanders Mansion, Carmel's need for a larger water allocation, and a planning commission resolution about ice cream parlors were all on the agenda.

Clint quickly realized that this was not a business. It was government, and there was no cutting through most of the bureaucracy to solve problems.

He was very strongly opposed to the city's spending of funds and excess time to study issues, something the previous administration did all the time. The term EIR stands for environmental impact report, but to Clint it must have seemed like "every inch of red tape!"

City Hall was too small for the droves of people who wanted to attend the council meetings, so the city leased the Carmel Women's Club, which could accommodate over 200 people. Many times the building was filled with tourists and residents who attended for a few minutes and then left.

The normally slow-paced Carmel Police Department with its sixteen sworn officers had two undercover detectives attend each council meeting. Detective Peter Poitras and Captain Donald Fuselier, who became Carmel's Chief of Police in

1993, were on hand in case there were incidents. Clint had been threatened on many occasions as an actor, and no one knew what to expect with his new proximity to the public.

Many women purposely came to Carmel to try to meet the mayor. Some sat in the front row of the council meetings and just stared at him. On one occasion, a woman spoke to him from the microphone and threatened suicide if he didn't pay attention to her. She was quickly removed.

Most people soon realized the meetings were not movies. They were as boring as other town meetings, but Clint's council allowed everyone to speak on the issues. It was a point he campaigned on. On only one occasion was Clint considered rude by cutting short the presentation of Jean Mayer, a long-time resident and Townsend supporter. The mayor said she had already given the talk four months before so he was justified in interrupting her.

A Monterey musical group called the Medflies capitalized on the mayor's fame by writing and performing a song called "Don't Mess With the Mayor!" It was a take-off on the theme song from *The Good, The Bad and the Ugly* which Clint had made years earlier.

Clint's council appointed Robert Evans as chairman of the General Plan Review Committee, which also included Olaf Dahlstrand, a former planning commissioner, Alan Williams, who was part of the original committee, Jean Grace, and Ed Hicks. Second kitchens became the hot topic for months. These units allowed, in many cases, senior citizens to rent out their own homes and live in a studio unit. A second unit law, authored by State Senator Henry Mello, allowed for these units. Carmel had objected to it under Townsend's administration. The issue continued until the 1988 city council approved an ordinance allowing the units.

During his administration, Clint had three government commissions: planning, forestry, and community and cultural, which included the recreation commissions. He also established a Mayor's Advisory Committee which consisted of Florence Berrey, Bill Ellis, Phyllis Howard, Howard Nieman, Jr., Bob Priestly, and Dorothea Roberts. The committee kept the mayor informed about town problems and made suggestions.

Clint opposed Townsend's general plan, especially regarding the zoning issue. Some areas of town had zoning differences within one block, or in his case, within one building where commercial and residential zoning conflicted. Townsend feared Carmel would lose its anti-growth stance if the plan wasn't approved. Her supporters said some members of the review committee, namely developer Alan Williams, were really self-serving by recommending changes that favored additional development.

Another zoning issue that caused controversy was the renting of private residences for short periods of time. Because the houses weren't zoned for commercial use, it was against the city's law to rent them for the weekend. In 1981 and 1982 Carmel-by-the-Sea passed several ordinances which made the renting of a home for thirty days or less a criminal offense. A 1982 Superior Court decision ruled the ordinances to be unconstitutional at that time. The issue came to the forefront again in 1986 when a resident saw people going into a neighbor's house on a Friday, and leaving on Sunday with suitcases. The coming and going of different people every weekend aroused suspicion that the house was being used for commercial purposes. Talk about neighborhood watch! A law suit was filed by Ewing, et al, in 1989 against the City of Carmel-By-The-Sea. The ordinance was upheld in Superior Court. There were not to be any short-term rentals in the residential district unless specific zoning was approved. Once again, residential interests have taken precedence over commercial ones as stated in the Magna Carta.

The Park Branch of the Harrison Memorial Library became a reality when Clint became directly involved and negotiated the purchase and business arrangements.

Carmel had little to offer its minimal youthful population until Clint's administration. Surfers were being targeted for their dressing into wet suits in front of houses on Scenic Drive and showing their naked bodies to the public. Skateboarders appealed to the new, friendly city council for a skateboard park. Clint equipped the weight room at the Youth Center as he had done with the Robert Louis Stevenson School in Pebble Beach. Some equipment came from actor Arnold Schwarzenegger, and Joe Gold, the owner of a Southern California gym.

The parking garage feud came to a close under Clint's administration when the council approved a paved parking area at the Sunset Center. With Carmel's approximate annual $6 million budget,

about $1300 per person, there were no excuses for not having the facility. The only parking problem left to untangle was the one presented by delivery trucks blocking the narrow streets. To date, however, no parking garage structure has been built.

During Clint's administration, council member Helen Arnold became terminally ill. Because of this and for her work on the council, Clint appointed her to the position of vice mayor. Robert Evans, a good friend of Clint's, was later appointed to fill the vacancy on the council.

Elinor Laiolo was successful in convincing the city council to re-establish the Pledge of Allegiance at each council meeting.

After hosting a major benefit party for the Forest Theater Guild where plans for its renovation were revealed on TV to the community, I made a formal presentation to the city council requesting additional funds to complete the project. Clint, the actor, understood the importance of the theater, and the council knew its historical significance as a community activity which had provided residents and tourists with so much entertainment over the years. The council voted to appropriate matching funds for the project.

An organization called Friends of the Sunset Center, chaired by Gordon Paul Smith, approached the city with plans for renovation of the building that included underground parking. Virginia Stanton, the peninsula's well-known philanthropist, offered the city $1 million to complete the project. Residents complained in fear that if there was expansion and renovation, more tourists and cars would come to Carmel. It sounded rather like the movie *Field of Dreams;* if there was expansion, more would come. The town often tries hard to ignore the significance of tourists, but it is those people who purchase goods, stay in hotels, eat in restaurants, and add to Carmel's financial base.

There was also concern that an enlarged facility might not be used enough to pay for it. The term *white elephant* became an argument against this change. Clint polled the residents with a postcard survey, one of many he personally paid for during his term in office. The residents said no and so did the council.

In 1992, however, the issue of renovating the center surfaced again. This time, there were no offers from private donors. The city council chose to hire experts to study the issue and a decision was still pending in 1993.

Six months after the election, it appeared that opinions were divided about Clint's term in office thus far. Many residents thought he was trying to act too quickly. Clint thought city government should act and do things for the citizens, not keep from solving problems. The city had used 99.97 percent of its annual water allotment and the Monterey Peninsula Water Management District Board could have stopped the water meters if it had reached 100 percent.

Residents were pleased when Carmel imposed a water moratorium on the town which slowed down building. In fact, they bragged about how they couldn't wash their cars, or hose down their sidewalks. Clint said the council feared that if the Monterey Peninsula Water Management District

imposed a moratorium, they wouldn't know how to get out of it. Carmel had a lawsuit pending against the water board claiming the city's allotment placed the district board in the business of land use planning. It also claimed the original allotments were not accurate. They did not consider renovations such as adding bathrooms, or new development.

His foes even criticized the types of tourists who came to town only to buy a pastry or ice cream after the gellatto shop opened, and those who only came to watch the mayor at council meetings. Clint said that in the end the people would ultimately evaluate his term of office when it was over, but he felt that more citizens were getting involved and willing to speak up at meetings.

The town really doesn't have any crime to speak of, except for the occasional minor crimes like shoplifting and residential burglaries. There were two murder-suicides, however; one in 1991 and another in 1993, both of which shocked the quiet town. Minor violations, of course, include the innumerable parking tickets given to tourists by the very active ticket writers who seem to appear from the trees. Carmel does not have parking meters. Instead, there are time limits.

Occasionally, the mayor practiced with the Carmel officers at the shooting range, which kept morale up and the officers interested in the town and politics. Clint wanted the police to take a more friendly approach to the town and its citizens rather than a hard-line stereotypical one. He even suggested that the officers wear something other than blue uniforms.

The Carmel Beach Restoration Project along

Scenic Drive turned into another hotly-contested issue, only this time the major conflicts turned up in the council itself. Originally, the discussion was about restoration of the beach and cliffs above it. Jean Grace chaired the review committee for the project. Councilwoman Elinor Laiolo sometimes annoyed Clint with her pursuit of the details and outspoken opinion, which appeared to slow down the decision-making process, especially on this walkway issue.

The project called for a landscaped walkway and stairways to the beach and the removal of about 42 of nearly 150 parking spaces on Scenic Drive. The California Coastal Conservancy offered $250,000 of the total $750,000 cost to Carmel along with state grant funds and the city's funds, too. Laiolo feared Carmel would be giving up control to the state, and she even spoke at the Coastal Commission hearing. She was in favor of protection of the bluffs from water erosion, and supported the beach restoration itself, but not the added walkway which she determined was new development that eliminated several parking spaces on Scenic Drive. Citizens wrote op-ed pieces.

Clint countered by taking another postcard poll. The town responded positively to accept the walkway project and work began.

Carmel's Planning Commission was inundated with building-permit requests and many were granted. If a project needed additional water, however, the commission turned down the permit, upsetting many builders whose lenders were becoming concerned over delays. Those permits couldn't be forthcoming until Carmel received a larger water allocation. Even Clint's commercial building was on hold because of this water issue.

Carmel is certainly unique in its selective rules and regulations. Residents wander the streets at night with flashlights because there aren't any streets lights in the residential areas. This is supposedly in keeping with the forest ambiance. The town also legislates the amount of wattage on outdoor lighting of residences. The police recommend keeping houses well lit to deter crime, but crime prevention doesn't seem to take precedence over other matters in Carmel.

There is no live music allowed in Carmel. Residents go to the Mission Ranch piano bar for entertainment or the barn there which, for a while, had jazz nights. An ordinance limiting the height of women's high heels is still on the books in Carmel-by-the-Sea because the city won't accept liability for its non-existent to poorly-repaired sidewalks.

Mayoral candidate Timothy Grady started a recall of Eastwood in September 1986 when the mayor failed to oppose building the Inn at Spanish Bay in Pebble Beach. The recall never got off the ground, however.

Carmel has also battled with the California State Transportation District over the Hatton Canyon Freeway since 1947. The man originally assigned to that project, Ken Jones, said he would probably retire before it was resolved, and in fact he did. Drivers on Highway One encounter 15-minute delays from just south of Carmel northward to Monterey because the highway forms two lanes instead of four. The issue of either expanding Highway One or building the freeway east of the current highway is in direct opposition to those who believe that saving trees and wildlife along the proposed route is more important.

Once a month, the Mayors Select Committee, which was really the Monterey Peninsula mayors, held an "old boys network" luncheon. When Clint left office, one mayor said he missed those talks with Clint more than anything else. The mayors honored the actor and their colleague by saying he was a "regular guy."

Late in 1986, Clint purchased the Mission Ranch which pleased Helen Arnold and Helen Wilson, two women who were active in Carmel's historic preservation. In 1993, the Carmel Heritage Society honored Clint for keeping the ranch from commercial development.

Clint has always been a philanthropist, giving of his time and money to causes he believes in over the years. For example, he donated the proceeds from a televised "roast," given by the Variety Club International of Los Angeles, to Monterey's Youth Recovery Program, where young people were treated for drug and alcohol abuse.

On October 3, 1987, King Juan Carlos of Spain visited Monterey and met with Clint at the official opening of the Clint Eastwood Youth Recovery Program. Elinor Laiolo had the distinction of escorting Juan Carlos through Carmel during his visit.

Clint appeared at dinners and major benefits throughout his term of office, including one for Friends of the Big Sur Coast, which was raising money to counter attempts at making Big Sur into a National Scenic Area. Eastwood had opposed national scenic designation, but as a Big Sur property owner, and as a member of Carmel's City Council he abstained from any final vote fearing conflict-of-interest charges. In July 1986, however, I represented Carmel in Washington, D.C. at a senate hearing on the issue, not only with Clint's approval but with a letter from a majority of Carmel's city council members. The senate committee ultimately voted against making Big Sur a national scenic area.

THE IRONY OF IT ALL

Could there be a better turn of plot than having David Maradei come before Clint's council to appeal for a building height variance?

The community waited and wondered how fair Clint would be under the circumstances. He showed his clout, no doubt about it. Maradei and Judith Wolfe, co-owners of a Carmel residence, stood before the council with their request before them. They needed to extend the roof line higher than the city's normal allowance would permit.

The mayor didn't waste time. He began by reading the same letter which Maradei and Helen Arnold sent him when they sat on the city council and voted against Clint's variance. In the end, however, Clint proved to be a gentleman and abstained from voting because of his potential prejudice.

When the council members Fischer, Laiolo, and Evans, denied the request, Maradei's friends charged Clint again with attempting to seek revenge. Wright, whom Clint called the "lone wolf" because he had no support on the council, cast the sole dissenting vote. Clint had his ironic day.

Whomever was voting on these issues, though, the lesson was clear. If you want to build in Carmel, be prepared for the long haul. It's an endurance test. Even putting an awning over a business can take years. One recent applicant for a residential building permit has waited two years and said once he gets it, he'll sell the property, never to return again. Two years? One of California's most prominent families has waited eleven years.

THE ALBATROSS

Eastwood knew that Carmel had been unfairly allocated water by the Monterey Peninsula Water Management District Board when the original allotments were made. There was no provision for renovations let alone new development.

For months after Clint was elected, many residents attended the Water Board meetings and appealed for a greater water allowance. One of those was Alan Williams, who had development projects on hold because no water permits were being approved. Clint couldn't even build his own building. The area was experiencing a drought. There was the added possibility of rationing and increased water rates, which occurred later anyway.

The Board was in control of the Peninsula cities and worked on a budget of about $2 million per year. The Board was mandated by the California Legislature to find additional sources of water. It hadn't done so.

Although Carmel had filed a lawsuit against the Monterey Peninsula Water Management District, the water issue had come to a standstill, until the fall of 1986 when I called Clint in Los Angeles.

(He often commuted from his Los Angeles office throughout his two-year term.)

I suggested that I contact State Senator Henry Mello, who sponsored the legislation that had made the water board a reality. Clint was delighted that a new idea might help. I arranged a meeting betwen Mello and Eastwood. The senator enjoyed meeting the actor and an instant rapport was established. That was the first of many behind-the-scenes meetings with the senator, members of his legislative staff and others as the months went on, and the beginning of technical research and liaison I provided on the water controversy.

A meeting of the mayors, county supervisors, and the senator was arranged in January 1987. Clint was so pleased at that meeting that he even served me a cup of tea. There were many private meetings between the Senator and the water board's manager, Bruce Buehl, who was highly criticized for the number of studies conducted without results over the years.

KSBW-TV, an NBC affiliate, was very receptive when I proposed and developed a television program about the water issue that would provide viewers throughout the broadcast area in several counties with information about the peninsula's water shortage problem. The panel of experts who appeared on the show included Senator Mello, Clint, water board chairman Dick Heuer, and a member of the Sierra Club, Dale Hekheuis. The prime-time program allowed an open discussion about the issue. Eastwood liked the idea that action was being taken and that there was the potential of solving this vexing problem.

It was this issue that occupied most of Clint's time during his term of office. Hours each day were spent discussing how Carmel could obtain a larger water allocation. Such discussion brought out Eastwood's seldom-seen passion for politics.

During the next water district election campaign, Eastwood openly supported three candidates who favored building the much-discussed San Clemente Dam project, which could solve the water-shortage problems for everyone. Those three candidates were Paul Davis, a Monterey architect, James Hughes, a dentist from Pacific Grove, and Sandra Skillicorn, an accountant and wife of Carmel's treasurer, Jack Skillicorn.

In order to involve Pebble Beach residents, I coordinated a special party at a private Pebble Beach residence for 400 guests who were given the opportunity to meet the three candidates at a wine and cheese buffet. The six peninsula mayors (including Clint) all attended, and each made a brief speech after I introduced them. I deliberately introduced Clint last to keep the guests' attention.

Clint spent several thousand dollars of his own money for television ads in favor of the three candidates. In the end, Davis and Hughes were elected but Skllicorn wasn't. Most people agreed it was an improvement because the candidates were pro-dam. There were others who feared that more pro-dam members sitting on the board would mean that a dam *would* be built, resulting in loss of natural habitat for plants, fish, and wildlife.

In June 1987, I was invited to attend a meeting in Sacramento that included Senator Mello; Pete Bonattelli, the director of the State Fish and Game Department; members of the Peninsula Water District board; Nick Lombardo, who owns Rancho Canada, a Carmel Valley golf course; Dick Heuer, a member of the board; and the board's executive director, Bruce Buehl. The purpose was to discuss the possible commitments by the Fish and Game Department relating to the proposed dam and fish hatcheries.

It would be months, however, before any results were forthcoming. There were more discussions, private meetings, and presentations at water board meetings. Because of so much lobbying, most of it behind the scenes, and compounded by the pressure of another of Carmel's infamous lawsuits against the water board, Carmel was granted 100 extra acre-feet of water. Clint was credited with this accomplishment. He not only made everyone's day but their houses a possibility, too. After Clint left office, building began on many of the projects that had been waiting for water permits.

There was development of new homes and renovation of older ones. They seemed to happen at once, with the old cries that Clint was really a developer all along.

With Carmel's water problem temporarily in hand, the peninsula was still debating a dam. But with an ocean in front of it, and even with board changes and lobbying, the peninsula, to date, has not made progress in building a dam. In a desperate attempt to solve the problem for everyone, including his own future projects, Clint offered a portion of his Carmel Valley Canada Woods property as the site of a reservoir. After study, the idea was rejected because the property has a fault line running through it. Since that time, reclamation projects for Pebble Beach have been discussed so that reclaimed water could be used for irrigation of golf courses.

In 1992, a grand jury recommended the water board be disbanded because it had spent more than $20 million and had not completed its mandate, but the board was still active in 1993.

If there was one matter that frustrated Clint throughout his term of office, it was the water issue. He was used to quietly saying "action" while directing, sometimes without words, just eye movement or with his hands. Actors and production crew members responded accordingly. It wasn't so simple on this issue or any other political one.

THE END OF AN ERA

For many months, without the residents being aware of it, Clint was deciding whether he would run for a second term. His accomplishments during his two years in office were many. Everyone expected him to run again. But his family and friends had seen less of him since his election, and there was his movie career to think about, too. He had starred in only one movie; normally he made two per year.

When he discussed the matter with me, I said no matter how many years he served, whether two or twenty-two, people wouldn't appreciate him any more or less than they did right then. I saw Clint change from that first forum in 1986 when he was a nervous and novice candidate. I respected the mayor for his accomplishments. We had worked well together because we wanted to solve Carmel's prob-

lems. He had always been open to my suggestions, and entrusted me with his confidence and friendship. Never in my dreams could I have imagined advising a man of Clint Eastwood's stature, but politics has a strange way of bringing people together.

He opened his mind and heart to the people of Carmel-by-the-Sea and it showed on his face and the way he spoke. Not everyone was pleased with his administration. As accustomed to reviews as he has been during his thirty-nine years in movies, criticism still stung. Clint may have earned a reputation for being a "macho" character on screen, but he is also an intelligent and sensitive man. However, if he didn't run again, the question shifted to who could continue his policies.

Before Clint announced his decision, I suggested that he give the local NBC affiliate, KSBW-TV, an exclusive interview that would give him an opportunity to express his opinions about his term as mayor. The station's president, Jeffery Lee, and news director, Michael Kronley, were extremely cooperative as they had been during the campaign. After rounds of discussion with parameters agreed upon, the show was taped on the evening of January 28, 1988. There were no edits. It was live to tape. The half-hour program aired during prime time on January 31 without commercial interruption.

Clint was asked if he would run again and he avoided the answer by saying he would "make a decision next week." He said that although he had been highly criticized by many residents for what appeared to them as being pro-business, he would be the last person in the world to be so. He moved to Carmel to get away from the big-city atmosphere. "I have less motivation than anyone to be pro-development," he said.

On February 2, 1988, Al Eisner, the former owner of the *Carmel Pine Cone* and friend of David Maradei, took out a paid ad which recommended that Clint not run again because his pro-business attitude had alienated so many residents that he wouldn't win by such a wide margin. It didn't matter. Even though Clint hadn't made it public yet, his decision was made long before that ad ran.

On February 4, 1988 during the AT&T golf tournament, Mayor Clint Eastwood announced to Carmel and the world that he wouldn't seek another term of office. He said he wanted to spend more time with his two children. He was also in post-production on his movie, *Bird,* and about to start his next movie, *The Dead Pool.*

The filing deadline was extended until February 11, and almost immediately Clayton Anderson and Paul Laub declared their candidacies. Elinor Laiolo was considering running, but she still had two years to serve on the council. She could continue to carry out the policies established by Clint's mayoral term of office. Clint supported Jean Grace as his successor.

An organization called the Carmel Residents Association, or CRA, which was supported by Charlotte Townsend and her followers, also supported Grace. Clayton Anderson was a member of another group called the Northeast Neighborhood Association. These groups were blamed for all the political unrest in town.

Clayton Anderson made derogatory remarks about Grace's friendship with Clint. Shortly thereafter, the *National Enquirer* made calls to several area people. Local photographer and Carmel resident John Livingston was contacted for a photo of Clint and Grace. Clint approved the photo which appeared in a front page story of the tabloid on May 17, 1988. The photograph showed Clint shaking Grace's hand as she took office. It seemed that Carmel would always be in the national news. While Grace wore sunglasses for weeks attempting to draw attention away from the exploitive article that romantically linked the pair, Clint was denying any such relationship.

Several times during Clint's last city council meeting on April 5, 1988, he fell into laughter and put his head on the desk. The meeting agenda looked like it was going to be another marathon, but Clint was able to complete the meeting in three hours. He told everyone it was hard to be a mayor even though it may have looked easy. When a phone rang loudly in the room, he said it was probably his agent calling! The people in attendance were finally treated to a show. It was a "wrap." Now he could return to his own lifestyle once again.

FULL CIRCLE

After the 1988 election, Clint's restaurant, the Hog's Breath, was closed by the Monterey County Environmental Health Director, Walter Wong, who cited too many violations to name here. Clint hired Alan Williams to make the repairs. It was the first time that Williams candidly addressed his alliance with Clint as "we." The restaurant reopened within two weeks, and many said Clint was the brunt of a personal attack.

Clint told me he would withdraw from everything and take the advice he had given me by staying behind the scenes. He became a director in another sense, however, when he and some members of the original group who met prior to his 1986 election met again and formed a citizens group. He became a board member of the Citizens for Good Government along with Howard Nieman, Jr., Phyllis Howard, and Robert D'Isidoro. That organization wanted Carmel's council to become fiscally responsible and listen to the citizens.

Although Clint was spending more time now in Los Angeles than in Carmel, preparing for his next movie, *White Hunter Black Heart,* he wouldn't forget Carmel. In 1990 Elinor Laiolo chose to run for mayor against the incumbent Jean Grace. Clint, once again, after being caught in the middle between the two women, chose to support Grace again. Although a good percentage of the residents respected Laiolo's dedication to the town and her earnest decision-making, she lost to Grace.

Whether the town changed drastically during Clint's term of office remains a matter of opinion. But if it moved forward, it moved backward during Grace's administration and Ken White's.

Stella Biason, who donated the historic Murphy House to the town, fully understood what other residents had talked about in previous years. She donated the Murphy House because she would have needed a zoning change in order to use it for any other purpose. Her property had three buildings on it. Two were already in use and she hoped the third would be a place for an artist-in-residence who would paint on the premises. Even after her generosity, Biason's permit request was turned down. Imagine an artist being unwelcomed in

Carmel. The town had come full circle from the Eastwood administration.

Grace chose not to run again in 1992. Her administration had been highly criticized for spending too much money for property near the Mission Ranch. In fact, Clint declared Carmel "broke" in 1992 because the council had overspent its budget for property it couldn't afford.

Clint didn't develop any property until he was well out of office. In 1992 his commercial building was completed, and that same year he began the development process for the Carmel Valley ranch property he once offered as the site of a dam. Remember, he never denied being a developer.

In 1992, another CRA supporter, Ken White, was about to run unopposed for the office until Barney Laiolo, at the age of 83, ran against him because he said people should have a choice.

Laiolo didn't really campaign and spent only $800 while White spent about $8,000. Laiolo lost the election by about 150 votes. Imagine if he had made an all-out effort to win. There was thunderous applause in appreciation of Laiolo's efforts.

In fact, the Carmel City Council approved honoring Laiolo by erecting a placard along the Mission Trail. When the vote was taken on November 2, 1993, the city council debated whether it could honor someone who was still living. Headlines in the *Carmel Pine Cone* read "Council honors Barney Laiolo but not without a little fuss."

On June 8, 1993, 56.3 percent of Carmel's registered voters turned out for one of the most highly contested ballot measures in the town's history, Measure H. This ballot measure placed commercial

Mayor Clint Eastwood greets King Juan Carlos of Spain at the Monterey Youth Program's headquarters. Courtesy of the *Monterey Peninsula Herald.*

zoning interests against residential ones regarding a change in Carmel's commercial zone, which would extend the commercial zoning boundary line to 7th Street, south of Ocean Avenue.

Clint stepped forward and took an active role by coming out in favor of the measure. He spent $42,000 of his own money to support the issue. He directly involved himself with two groups, Yes for Carmel and as chairman of "Friends of Carmel," which supported the issue. He was, of course, highly criticized for using his clout and money to push through a measure that passed by only 10 votes. Councilwoman Barbara Livingston called Clint a "control freak," claiming that he wanted to control not only people but the town's issues, too.

In fact, the vote was so close that the Monterey County Registrar of Voters required a recount. There was no change in the final count. Mayor Ken White has already proposed changes to the measure.

Carmel's political history proves that the town does come together, if in no other way than to vote. And with people like Bert Heron, Clint Eastwood, and Barney Laiolo to speak for it, Carmel has been lit by a star or two.

from "Spring in Carmel"

On the emerald hills of Carmel the spring and
    winter have met.
Here I find in a gentled spot
The frost of the wild forget-me-not,
And—I cannot forget.

GEORGE STERLING

Acknowledgments

For assistance with the research for this book, the author gratefully acknowledges the many wonderful friends and residents who have assisted her efforts, including Margye Neswitz, Barney Laiolo, Elinor Laiolo, Bill Brown, publisher of the *Carmel Pine Cone,* and Associate Editor Lewis Leader of the *Monterey Peninsula Herald.*

For permission to reproduce their art, the author thanks artists Jim Miller of the Jim Miller Gallery in Carmel, Bill Dodge of the Dodge Gallery in Carmel, Bill Bates, and photographers Philip Neswitz, Will Wallace, Richard Bucich, and Kathleen Olson. For assistance with specific research the author wishes to acknowledge The Monterey Public Library Reference and California Room staff; the Boulder, Colorado Public Library reference staff, especially Judy Waller, Constance Walker, and Lynn Reed; Hank Ketcham, Gordon Greene, and Cole Weston; Carmel's Harrison Memorial Library and the Carmel History Room personnel; Mayo Hays O'Donnell Library; the Bancroft Library at the University of California, Berkeley; The Monterey History and Art Association; the Carmel History and Art Association; Tor House Foundation; the University of Colorado at Boulder Norlin Library reference staff; the University of Colorado Earth Sciences Library staff; the Pebble Beach Company public relations and archival staff, especially Diane Stracuzzi, Elmer Lagorio, and Elinor Lagorio; Gabriella Knubis; the Diocese of Monterey; the Monterey Bay Aquarium; the Robert Louis Stevenson School; the Marine Hopkins Library; the Monterey Peninsula Museum of Art; the Monterey Peninsula Chamber of Commerce; the Pebble Beach Post Office staff; the Monterey County Film Commission; Richard Andelson and the Steinbeck Arthurian Society; Isabelle Hall, and the Center for Marine Conservation.

For permission to reprint Henry Miller's quote from *Big Sur and the Oranges of Hyieronimous Bosch* in Chapter III, the author acknowledges New Directions Publishing Corporation.

Bibliography

Adams, Ansel, with Mary Street Alinder. *An Auto-biography*. Boston: Little Brown, 1985.

Baer, Morley, with Wallace David Rains. *The Wilder Shore*. San Francisco: Sierra Club, 1984.

Bahr, Robert. *Least Of All Saints*. New Jersey: Prentice Hall, 1979.

Benediktsson, Thomas E. *George Sterling*. Boston: G. K. Hall and Twayne Publishers, 1980.

Berger, John A. *The Franciscan Missions of California*. New York: Doubleday ,1941.

Bostick, Daisy F. and Dorothea Castelhun. *Carmel At Work and Play*. Monterey: Angel Press, 1977.

Breschini, Gary S. *The Indians Of Monterey County*. Carmel: Monterey County Historical Society, 1972.

Brower, David. *Not Man Apart*. New York: Ballantine, 1965.

Carmel Art Association. *Botke, McComas-Seideneck*. Carmel: Art Association, 1988.

Carpenter, Frederick I. *Robinson Jeffers*. New York: Twayne Publishers, Inc., 1962.

Castellanos, Emilio Carranza. *The Russian Invasion of California*. San Antonio: Freymann & Associates, 1984.

Chapman, Charles, Ph. D. *A History of California, The Spanish Period*. New York: MacMillan, 1921.

Cronise, Titus Fey. *The Natural Wealth of California*. California: H. H. Bancroft, 1868.

Dana, Richard. *Two Years Before The Mast*. New York: Dodd Mead & Co., 1946.

Drizari, Nelo. *Picturesque Garden of Enchantment*. Carmel By The Sea: Publishers Research Features.

Drury, Aubrey. *Point Lobos State Reserve*. California: The Resources Agency, 1975.

Dutton, Davis. *Missions of California*. New York: Westways, Ballantine, 1972.

Ferguson, Robert. *Henry Miller, A Life*. New York: W. W. Norton, 1991.

Ferlinghetti, Lawrence and Nancy J. Peters. *Literary San Francisco*. San Francisco: City Light Books and Harper & Row, 1980.

Fink, Augusta. *I-Mary, A Biography of Mary Austin*. Tucson: University of Arizona Press, 1983.

Fisher, Anne B. *No More A Stranger*. California: Stanford

University Press, 1946.

Fisher, Anne B. *The Salinas, Upside Down River*. Santa Cruz: Valley Publishers, 1945.

Ford, Tirey L. *Dawn and the Dons*. San Francisco: Bruce Brough Press, 1926.

Gebhard, David and Harriette Von Breton. *Architecture in California*. Santa Barbara: University of California, The Regents, 1968.

Hart, James D. *A Companion To California*. Berkeley: University of California Press, 1987.

Heizer, Robert F. *The Costanoan Indians*. Cupertino: California History Center, 1974.

Heizer, Robert F. and Albert B. Elazer. *The Natural World of the California Indians*. Berkeley: University of California Press, 1980.

Henny, Calvin. *James Fitzgerald*. Rockland: Wm. A. Farnsworth Library and Art Museum, 1984.

Howard, Donald M. *Primitives in Paradise, The Monterey Peninsula Indians*. Carmel: Antiquites Research Publications, 1975.

Jeffers, Donnan. *The Stones of Tor House*. California: Jeffers Literary Property, 1985.

Kenneally, Finbar OFM. *The Writings of Fermin Francisco de Lausen*. Washington, D.C.: Academy of American Franciscan History, 1965.

Kirker, Harold. *Old Forms on a New Land, California Architecture in Perspective*. Niwot, Colorado: Roberts Rinehart, 1991.

Kirker, Harold. *California's Architectural Frontier*. Salt Lake City: Gibbs M.Smith, Inc., 1960.

Knox, Maxine and Mary Rodriguez. *Making The Most Of The Monterey Peninsula and Big Sur*. San Rafael: Presidio Press, 1978.

Larkin, Thomas O. *Affair At Monterey*. Los Angeles: The Zamorow Club, 1964.

Lawson, Andrew. *The Geology of Carmelo Bay*. Berkeley: University of California Press, 1893.

Lydon, Sandy. *Chinese Gold, The Chinese in the Monterey Bay Region*. Capitola: Capitola Book Co., 1985.

Margolin, Malcolm. *The Journals of Jean Francois Galoup de La Perouse*. Berkeley: Heydey Books, 1989.

Margolin, Malcolm. *The Ohlone Way, Indian Life in the SanFrancisco-Monterey Bay Area*. Berkeley: Heydey Books, 1978.

Miller, Henry. *Big Sur and The Oranges of Hieronymous Bosch*. New York: New Directions Publishers, 1957.

McCoy, Esther. *Five California Architects*. New York: Reinhold Publishing Corporation, 1960.

McGlynn, Betty Hoag. *Art Association: A History,* Carmel Art Association. Carmel, CA., 1987.

McLane, Lucy Neely. *A Piney Paradise*. San Francisco: Lawton Kennedy, 1952.

Netland, Dwayne. *The Crosby—Greatest Show in Golf.* New York: Doubleday, 1975.

Osbourne, Lloyd. *An Intimate Portrait of Robert Louis Stevenson*. New York: Charles Scribners Sons, 1924.

Pike Donald. *Big Sur, The Greatest Meeting of Land and Sea*. Las Vegas: KC Publications, 1979.

Reinstedt, Randall A. *Ghosts, Bandits and Legends of Old Monterey, Carmel, and Surrounding Areas.* Carmel: Ghost Town Publications, 1974.

Reinstedt, Randall A. *Tales Treasures and Pirates of Old Monterey.* Carmel: Ghost Town Publications, 1976.

Risenberg, Felix, Jr. *The Golden Road, The Story of California's Spanish Mission Trail.* New York: McGraw-Hill, 1962.

Rolle, Andrew F. *California, A History.* 2nd Ed., New York: Thomas Crowell Company, 1969.

St. Johns, Adela Rogers. *Final Verdict.* New Jersey: Doubleday, 1962.

St. Pierre, Brian. *John Steinbeck, The California Years.* San Francisco: Chronicle Books, 1983.

Schmitz, Anne-Marie. *In Search of Steinbeck.* California: Hermes Publication, 1978.

Spangenberg, Helen. *Party Time On The Monterey Peninsula.* Monterey: Herald Printers, 1980.

Sterling, George. *Selected Poems of George Sterling.* New York: Henry Holt and Company, 1923.

Stevenson, Robert Louis. *From Scotland to Silverado.* Cambridge: Harvard University Press, 1966.

Sugden, John. *Sir Francis Drake.* New York: Henry Holt, 1990.

Temple, Sydney. *The Carmel Mission From Founding To Rebuilding.* Fresno: Valley Publishers,1980.

Thomas, Lately. *The Vanishing Evangelist, The Aimee Semple McPherson Kidnapping Trial.* New York: Viking, 1959.

Tibesar, Antonine, Ed. *The Writings of Junipero Serra.* Vols. I and III,Washington, D.C.: Academy of American Franciscan History, 1955.

Verardo, Jennie Dennis and Denzil. *The Salinas Valley, An Illustrated History.* Windsor Publications, 1989.

Walker, Franklin. *The Seacoast of Bohemia.* California: Peregrine Smith, 1973.

Weston, Cole. *Fifty Years.* Utah: Gibbs Smith, 1991.

Whitcomb, Michael. *Carmel, The Architectural Spirit.* Carmel By The Sea: Ridgewood Press, 1978.

Wise, Winifred E. *Fray Junipero Serra And The California Conquest.* New York: Scribners, 1967.

Woodbridge, Sally B. *California Architecture, Historic American Building Survey.* San Francisco: Chronicle Books, 1968.

Woolfenden, John. *Big Sur, A Battle For The Wilderness 1869–1981.* Pacific Grove: Boxwood Press, 1981.

Index

Index

Index

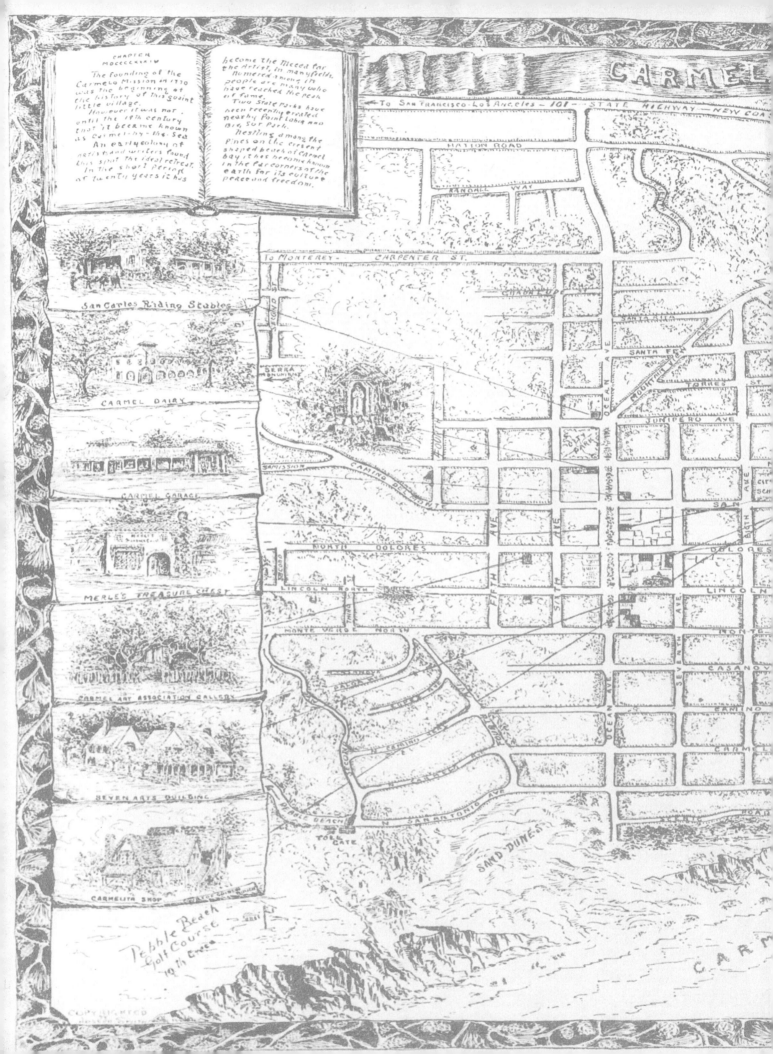